MAKING IT THROUGH
THE NAZI YEARS

MAKING IT THROUGH THE NAZI YEARS

Memoirs of Peter and Inge van Kessel

ROBERT J. VAN KESSEL

iUniverse, Inc.
New York   Bloomington

iUniverse books may be ordered through booksellers or by contacting:

iUniverse
1663 Liberty Drive
Bloomington, IN 47403
www.iuniverse.com
1-800-Authors (1-800-288-4677)

ISBN: 978-1-4401-9772-7 (pbk)
ISBN: 978-1-4401-9773-4 (ebk)

Printed in the United States of America

iUniverse rev. date: 02/11/2010

Contents

Acknowledgments

As with all my prior writing projects, I acknowledge my wife, Maria, whose patience and support is simply vast. I spent countless hours on the manuscript of this book which she knows has been a labour of love for me.

I am grateful to my siblings who read earlier drafts and offered their contributions and recollections of things our parents told them over the years.

I specially acknowledge Elaine Riehm, a long time family friend, who edited the final draft of this memoir.

Most importantly, I acknowledge my parents, Peter and Inge, who dredged up parts of their past lives to enrich our own.

Dedication

I dedicate this book to my siblings Jack, Peter, Marilyn, Linda and Wendy. It has fortified me to write this book and I hope it will do the same for you and your children when you read it and pass it down through the generations.

Preface

To gather information for their story of survival, I interviewed my parents, now in their eighties, made them remember what they could and, perhaps, what they had intentionally forgotten about World War II and life under Nazi occupation in Holland. I also drew on my late grandfather's writings about his dramatic five-day battle with Nazis forces to defend Holland from invasion in May, 1940. I was fortunate my father kept "postcard" images of Rotterdam taken before and just after the invasion which show the devastation inflicted on the city.

Introduction

For my parents, Petrus (Peter) van Kessel and Ingetje (Inge) Schiebaan, who were born in Holland in the mid-1920s, the Nazi Years actually began in the 1930s with Hitler's ascent to power. They experienced the rise and reach of Nazism in Germany and Holland at first subtly as young kids during the Great Depression and then with growing intensity as teenagers when German armed forces invaded their country on May 10, 1940. For the next five years their families, and many others, barely coped with the scarcity, fear and tension that life under German and Dutch Nazi occupation entailed.

In May 1944, just after he finished high school in Rotterdam, German authorities ordered Peter to report for forced labour deployment to serve the Nazi war effort. He did not comply. Instead, Peter's father arranged to send him underground to avoid enslavement in Germany. But, two months later on a secret visit to Rotterdam to see Inge, he was betrayed. In the middle of the night, the police arm of the Dutch Nazi Party arrested him at gun point in Inge's home and took him away.

Over the next five months Peter lived a nightmare of Nazi interrogations and threats, solitary confinement, concentration camp and slave labour until he escaped from barbed wire confinement near the city of Arnhem on Christmas Day, 1944. On his trek back to Rotterdam, snipers shot at Peter as he furtively walked through a landing zone used by the Allies during the famous *Battle of Arnhem* four months earlier. He evaded German soldiers by blending into the background and survived ten incredible heart-pounding seconds of terror that, once again, brought him within an inch of his life. During his escape run Peter was unaware that Inge and his only sister, Truus, had risked their lives desperately trying to find him.

This memoir is set against the backdrop of events foretelling the tide of war ---the invasion and occupation of Holland and the battle for the liberation of Europe. The story begins with the Peter and Inge's early years and the spectre threatening to sweep over Europe during the 1930s.

Chapter One

Early Years and the Tide of War

Peter was born in 1925 on a living room table in a small ordinary tenement in the North Sea port city of Rotterdam. Before him came his brother Piet, then the twins, Jan and Jaap, and, lastly, his baby sister Truus. In the early 1930s when he was a young boy, Peter recalls that Hitler was spoken of as the "saviour of Germany." He heard this from a few people though he cannot remember exactly from whom. However, it is the truth, that is how the Germans viewed *Der Fuhrer* whom they elected Reichs Chancellor in 1933. They worshipped him like a god. Hitler was all about discipline, authority and the greatness of the Aryan race---and the inferiority of others.

Peter's father, Jacob, a man born in 1900 into a strict Calvinist family, was also a disciplinarian who thrived on exerting authority as a teacher, a lieutenant in the army reserves and a parent. He inflicted corporal punishment on his children at home when he felt it necessary to do so or because their mother, Elizabeth, reported their misbehaviour to him, an inevitable occurrence whenever she would say "Wait till your father gets home." When she said that there was no discussion, and no explanation would suffice to avoid the punishment. In his early school years Peter attended the primary school where Jacob taught Math and French and therefore had to behave well at school or his father would quickly find out about it and Peter could pay the price---the wooden spoon or, worse, the *matteklopper* (an instrument used to beat dust from rugs and discipline into children!).

Accentuating the austerity at home, this period was also the height of the Great Depression, which was by no means the first one Holland and Europe had experienced. Those of 1850, 1870 and 1900 were just as severe, if not more so, at a time when there was less public support and fewer resources available. During this particular depression, as with the prior ones, men were unemployed in large numbers. There were many apartments for sale or for rent in Peter's neighbourhood. Idle forlorn-looking men, young and old, walked the streets aimlessly looking for jobs that were not there, while hungry children toddled about. It was a time of sadness, want and shortages for many city residents that, retrospectively, however, was a picnic compared to the conditions of city life that plagued the Dutch during the war.

As a teacher Jacob had a good job, and the buying power of his salary in guilders increased as prices steadily dropped. Thus, the family was able to afford a few things such as holidays that many others could not. For several years during the summers of the early 1930s Peter's family spent a month on the freezing beaches along the North Sea coast near Katwijk, not far from The Hague. Jacob rented the house of a local fisherman who, together with his family, moved out for the duration. As the water temperature in the North Sea rarely got above sixteen degrees Celsius, swimming often did not last long, and it was windy all the time. The nearby dikes along the shore line were like earthen dams and had been started by the Romans two thousand years ago. That part of Holland, including Rotterdam, is part of a large delta where the Rhine and Maas rivers flow into the North Sea. Dikes were a common part of Holland's coastal topography long before the country was formed.

In 1933, Peter's home in Rotterdam was an apartment in a four-story building above a milk, cheese and egg shop located on a busy city street. The front entrance door of the building was right off a sidewalk and when the bell was rung, the door latch was pulled open by means of a long string from above. On the second floor of the apartment was a hallway with the kitchen at the end. The large living room had an old-fashioned coal burner and *faux* marble mantelpiece decorated with little angels blowing trumpets and looked out over an interior landscaped large courtyard ringed by small fenced gardens belonging to ground floor apartments. The space between the buildings was taken up by brick wide sidewalks on both sides and brick road pavement in between. At the young age of eight Peter did not read newspapers of course and he preferred to play outside whenever possible. However, as there were no playgrounds or green places he played soccer or other street games on the pavement with his buddies. Each block had its own "bobby" who walked the beat. As playing soccer on the street was prohibited, one of the boys had to be on the lookout.

By 1934 when Peter turned nine and Inge eight they occasionally heard more about how Hitler was transforming Germany. But to kids that age with no idea about politics it was just a name heard from time to time, though seemingly more often. At that time, Dutch radio broadcast mostly religious programs and church services that were not of much interest to Peter or Inge. Peter's parents, however, were quite religious while Inge's were less so. Elizabeth was raised as Dutch Reformed, a less intense form of the Calvinist protestant religion than the one (*Gereformeerde*) in which Jacob was indoctrinated. The family was made to go to church, initially twice on Sundays. No entertainment was allowed such as playing on the street or bicycling. There was a compulsory walk on Sunday afternoon to show off the twins which, when Jacob was there, was done mostly to make Elizabeth happy. Jacob would rather have been elsewhere---on an army base with his platoon pals where he was stationed as a reservist.

Peter recalls that at home some time in 1935 Jacob and his two younger brothers, Maurits and Pieter, along with colleagues and friends, discussed what was happening in Germany. It was generally said that Hitler put the Germans back to work building infrastructure---autobahns and railroad systems to move his army around---and producing weaponry. Peter recalls they talked about it in a positive way. That is certainly how the Germans saw it too. To the background of Hitler's booming rhetoric, munitions, armaments and other industrial factories were building up Germany's menacing military industrial complex and armed forces and thereby putting the populace back to work. By then, Hitler had rejected the 1919 Treaty of Versailles that arguably had hamstrung Germany so badly with war reparations and military constraints after its defeat in World War 1 that it gave him the platform he needed to persuade virtually all Germans (other than those who were non- Aryan) to get on board the Nazi express train. That year Hitler also created the *Luftwaffe* and introduced military conscription for all German men which further made his intentions obvious to his European neighbours.

During the summer of 1935, for the first time, Jacob took Peter and Piet on bicycles to camp in the Belgian Ardennes, a beautiful hilly countryside perhaps one hundred and sixty kilometres away from their home in Rotterdam. Over three days they rode bikes laden with camping gear while stopping along the way at places like Louvain and Poulseur in Belgium. Jacob's brother Maurits (whom Peter and Piet really liked) came along on that trip too. Peter remembers the brakes on his uncle's bike failing as he sped down a long hill with all the strapped on cooking equipment rattling and clattering as the pots and pans banged together. He will never forget the look of fear on his uncle's face while he held on for dear life. When Maurits got to the bottom of the hill, the relief on his face was clear. While Peter and Piet initially laughed at the awkward sight of their uncle noisily racing out of control down the hill, they soon realized that Maurits could have been seriously hurt had he fallen.

Eventually Maurits fixed up his bike and the group kept going. When they finally got to their destination, Jacob rented a small island in the river Ourthe accessible only by a boat pulled along a cable. The island was set against a large hill with a marble quarry at the top that looked very large to Peter. They had great fun catching little trout in the river using a glass bottle with the bottom knocked out using bread as bait. As there was no drinking or smoking in Peter's home (due to a long history of temperance in their religion), he and Piet were surprised to find a bottle of wine in the river where they camped; it seemed odd to them that it would be there. When they dutifully reported this to Jacob, he confessed to his sons that the bottle belonged to him and Maurits to be consumed at another time. Peter did not think it lasted very long---there was obviously some tolerance for alcohol! It was one of those examples of deviation from devotion to religious piety that immediately caused confusion and suspicion in Peter's mind.

The tranquillity of the Belgian Ardennes was legendary and drew many people for holiday and exploration. However, in just ten years the serenity and beauty of the area near where Peter camped with his father, brother and uncle would become the scene of a cataclysmic military encounter, the Battle of the Bulge, where German and Allied armies collided in December 1944 during Germany's last major ground offensive of World War II. Peter would be able to hear the distant sounds of that battle from where he was incarcerated near Arnhem. But, for Peter and Piet, who only had "having fun" on their young minds, real military battles were the furthest things from their thoughts.

In 1936, Jacob rented a six-passenger Chevrolet car that was really more like a small bus to go on another summer vacation. General Motors exported vehicles to countries in Europe including Holland, but few of them were around. He hired a mechanic chauffeur to do the driving---a friend of a friend who wanted to come on the trip if they fed him, which they did. The vehicle had a small trailer that they loaded up with luggage. The passengers were Jacob, Elizabeth, her baby brother Joop, their maid Kitty and two young ladies who were relatives. With their luggage loaded on top of the car and in a small trailer attached to the car with two leather belts off they went through countryside and village after village along small roads paved in bricks or cobblestones. Of course there were no large highways, so to speak, in those days and therefore it took a lot longer to get to places.

As Jacob was curious about conditions in Germany, the family crossed into Germany from Strasbourg, France, to see with their own eyes the miracle Hitler was performing there. Peter distinctly remembers passing through towns such as Freiburg in western Germany which proclaimed on bill boards in German "the Road to Palestine is not through this town!" They also met some Hitler youths wearing leather shorts called *Lederhosen* who wondered when they were going to join them, as if they had been told that Holland would soon seamlessly blend into Germany. Peter did not think too much about the question at the time; he did not yet fully appreciate that Hitler had done a good job mesmerizing that nation and building up the German spirit. It was well known in Europe that the Germans were highly susceptible to nationalism and knew how to follow and respect authority---and Hitler knew how to dish it out. The Dutch, too, had a Nazi party during the 1930s which sympathized with Hitler and glorified him and his policies. Its leader, Anton Mussert, organized the Dutch Nazis in Holland.

There were other military events in 1936 in addition to what Hitler was doing on Holland's doorstep that also foretold the tide of war. That year *Il Duce* Mussolini turned Ethiopia, Eritrea, and Somaliland into Italian East Africa. The Spanish Civil War also began under General Franco who, by 1938, controlled all of Spain. With military support, Hitler and Mussolini helped establish Spain as a totalitarian dictatorship. Spain joined the German and Italian "Axis" of which Japan, too, was a member. They were a conglomeration of dictatorships that the League of Nations (the predecessor to the United Nations) was impotent to do much about. Military muscle flexing and sabre rattling by a re-armed Germany and its allies was a growing threat to world peace.

As early as 1937, some friction existed within Peter's family between Jacob and Elizabeth's three brothers about what would happen in case of war with Germany. In that event Jacob felt there was no question the Dutch would have to fight; he was a patriot that way. Other countries such as France and England felt they would be wise to appease Hitler; the weak fool, British Prime Minister Neville Chamberlain, who became Prime Minister in 1937, being the most gullible of leaders willing to do that.

Meanwhile, as the war noise increased in 1937, Jacob built what might have been one of the first recreational vehicle trailers. He constructed it on a Chevrolet car using wood framing covered with steel sheathing and used it to take the family, except Truus, on another summer trip through the Belgian Ardennes to France. Upon arriving there, they inadvertently ended up camping in the Maginot Line, an immense barrier to invasion built starting in 1929 and named after France's war minister at the time. The line ran from Switzerland to Montmédy and had many underground fortifications and bunkers. The next morning they found out about their little breach when a French Army Patrol showed up to tell them to get the hell out of there as they were about to start shooting off grenades at a nearby firing range. The family promptly left of course.

Travelling along through France Peter's family crossed the Rhine River at Strasbourg into Germany where the Germans (again) welcomed them with open arms in an upbeat reception. That night they arrived late in Freiburg and camped in the city park without a permit, as the cops made clear to them early the next morning when they kicked them out. All these little transgressions added to the excitement of that trip!

Inge's family did not enjoy such family holidays outside Holland during the 1930s. Instead, her grandmother, Ingetje, who was reasonably well off because her husband had been a painter who owned a few properties before he died quite young, would rent a place along the Dutch coast where the family would go in the summer time to frolic along the North Sea beach in places like Katwijk, similar to how Peter's family had enjoyed summer breaks. There was discord between the grandmother and Inge's father, Aart, as he did not make much money and had to submit to living in his mother-in-law's home where she ruled the roost.

By 1937 Inge had become quite a good pianist though her lessons were stopped that year because she spent too much time on her bike. Fondly, she recalls a badly tuned piano in her home that she and a cousin often used when they put on plays. One of Inge's favourite piano pieces was the classic Waltz of Durand which her cousin Hans was also good at playing when he came to visit. Inge has been a pianist for over seventy years. She had the musical talent to become renowned but life---and war---intervened. She was a nice young girl whose transgressions were limited to begging for cigar bands on Friday nights (smoking cigars was very popular) for her collection and, one day that year while playing, she jumped through a hedge unexpectedly into the arms of the burgomaster (mayor) of the town where she lived. It was an innocent childhood act, but she has not forgotten the shock.

Peter, however, was a typical boy whose time outside school was spent hacking around with friends, visiting the busy harbour areas to see the large ships and the wares they brought to the docks and playing his most beloved sport---soccer. He remembers that sometimes he and his friends would play soccer even when it rained. As the ball was made from pretty basic leather it absorbed the moisture and gained a pound or two of water. When it struck one of them it was like being hit with a bag of concrete and a bruise or two was not uncommon. That did not matter, however, as he was not the kind of guy who would let that sort of thing stand in the way of playing the game. He was a tough kid who, when he was just five years old, saved the life of a two year toddler who had fallen into a ditch filled with water and deep, sticky mud. He would need to draw upon his innate sense of fortitude many times during the war.

By 1938, the signs of a looming war became rather clear, and that was what people generally talked about. In Peter's family, the talk always related back to Jacob and Elizabeth's memories of World War I, how the war was conducted then, how it would be different now, how Holland had avoided it, how it could avoid war this time and so on. Discussion in Inge's family about a possible war occurred only among the adults, and she has little memory of that sort of thing being discussed in her presence quite likely, she believes, to not worry her and her sisters. It was not something for women, let alone a twelve-year-old girl, to participate in. Inge's grandmother, Ingetje, lived upstairs in the same house and she taught Inge how to make soup (how the

Dutch love their soup!) and she was very strict about cleanliness. Inge was also crazy about *appelbollen* (apples wrapped in pastry) but getting that was a rarity in those days.

That year, there were also border incidents with Czechoslovakia that led Hitler to mass troops there, but France, Britain, and Soviet Russia held him back---at least for the moment. Hitler had said that he would attack Czechoslovakia unless that country ceded the Sudetenland (where a German minority resided) to the glorious Third Reich. He had said that if the Sudeten issues could be resolved he would not move on other countries in Europe. Though Hitler could not be trusted, on behalf of Great Britain, Chamberlain signed a treaty with Germany in 1938. He either could not read Hitler very well or was too weak to oppose him. As we all know, Hitler's ambitions did not end with Czechoslovakia---he was a liar of great magnitude. Elizabeth often used to say to her kids that, if they did not want to eat what she put on the table, "Some day you will want!" It was as if she prophesized what was coming with Hitler's then hidden goal of European, if not world, domination, and the horrible effects it would have on the Dutch in basic ways such as getting enough food to eat during the coming war years.

In the summer of 1938 Peter's family once more travelled to the Belgian Ardennes to camp, this time at a place called Houffalize, not far from Bastogne. On that trip they passed through Breda, Hasselt and Namen on the Meuse River---called the Maas River by the time it reaches Holland. There were no camp grounds in those days; people made a deal with a farmer, camped and enjoyed the countryside, in this case, the site of a very old grist mill located on a small stream. Coming from the city the kids loved it even though it was a three or four hour trip by car to get there. Jacob was able to afford vacations because the exchange rate for the Dutch guilder was advantageous with respect to the Belgian franc, the French franc and the German mark. For example, one of the first times Peter was in a restaurant was in Louvain (a town on the Meuse River). He had a whole speckled trout dinner with *frites* that cost the princely sum of one Belgian franc, a ridiculously cheap price in Dutch guilders.

Also in 1938, Hitler annexed Austria to Germany. Apparently Jacob was not surprised at this development, he expected it. Peter heard about the annexation through the radio program *Großdeutscher Rundfunk* and read about it in the newspaper. He wondered what might happen next! Later in August 1938 a German- Russian non-aggression pact was signed, but Stalin would soon find out what a liar Hitler was too, though do not have any sympathy for Stalin, who killed more of his own citizens than Hitler did and was just as psychotically brutal.

By February 1939, Hitler finally moved on Czechoslovakia professing (again) to protect the minority Sudeten Germans there---another pretext for aggression. Then, a month later, the German army strode into Prague as Czechoslovakia came under Nazi control through a treaty. It was obvious to everyone except Chamberlain that Hitler would have to be stopped, as all of Eastern Europe was under threat from his Third Reich ambitions. Peter often recalls that Hitler claimed in speeches or through propaganda that Germany needed *Lebensraum* or room to live---the rest of Europe be damned.

Then fourteen years old, the sense grew in Peter's mind that war was imminent, and he was not alone in that respect. In Inge's family it was the same as the issue of invasion became more intensely discussed by the adults. The Dutch had serious concerns about maintaining Holland's neutral status. In school that issue was often discussed openly among Peter and Inge's teachers. Whether the Nazis would allow the Netherlands to remain neutral as she had been during World War I was topmost in the mind of Dutch citizens. But things went on as normally as possible because there was no other choice. Though how would it be possible for the Netherlands to remain neutral? All the countries around Holland would be at war and, within Peter and Inge's families, no one could imagine Nazi Germany respecting its neutrality. Jacob, as a first lieutenant in the Army reserves, expected to be called up as soon as the Dutch mobilized if and when hostilities started.

After Peter met Inge in 1942, she often told him about a friend named Irma who had a German mother and a Dutch father. Irma's father had a little car, a Fiat, and Inge and Irma drove with him one day in 1939 in his wee car. She had to sit in the back seat and Irma in the front passenger seat. They noticed a lot of Dutch soldiers marching in the streets and it was a scary atmosphere. As it was also a grey rainy day it was a sad and depressing sight to watch militarization through the drops of water cascading down the car's windows. Because they lacked military preparedness, the Dutch knew they were helpless to stop the Nazis if they invaded, but they would not go down immediately without a fight.

To add to the misery and worry, there were also border incidents with Germany which Peter and Inge heard about. One incident happened at Venlo, a town in the province of Limburg on Holland's southeast border with Germany. It involved the kidnapping by the Gestapo of two British Secret Service Agents. The Dutch agent who was with them at the time was shot dead by Gestapo agents disguised as anti-Hitler sympathizers. It was a further sign of things to come.

In the summer of 1939, Jacob was engaged in army exercises near Woudenberg in the province of Utrecht. There, he rented a farm house on a working farm where the family spent a good part of the summer. He was away during the days and only came home at night and never spoke about what he did. Peter got stung by many bees that summer when walking in furrows behind horse drawn ploughs, but to "city folk," the countryside was special, and he and his siblings loved it regardless of little nuisances---or whether Jacob was there. Of course, they could not know then that July and August of 1939 would be their last innocent summer for the next five years. Their trepidation increased as Nazi Germany flexed its military muscles more and more.

Then it happened: on September 1, 1939, Hitler's invasion of Poland from East Prussia, Pomerania, Silesia and Slovakia was in all the newspapers and on radio. Primarily reliant on their tanks, the German invasion was lightning quick and deadly---*Blitzkrieg* (lightning war). A couple of days later Britain and France declared war on Germany. Just two weeks after that on September 17, Russia hit Poland's eastern border taking control of its oil fields, though the Allies did not declare war on Russia, a clear example of a military double standard if ever there was one. On September 28, the foreign ministers of Germany and Russia, von Ribbentrop and Molotov respectively, divided up a hapless Poland.

Holland mobilized its army in early September 1939, and Jacob was called up from the reserves and stationed near Katwijk. This was the location of the North Sea beaches where his family, and Inge's family, often spent their summer vacations in the early 1930s. It was also near the Valkenburg Airfield where Jacob eventually fought the Germans in May 1940. He remained at his army base until the Christmas holidays and then returned to Katwijk where he stayed in barracks for the next seven months conducting military drills and exercises. As far as Peter knows, Jacob did not communicate with his family at all in that period---another one of those long absences for which little, if any, explanation was ever forthcoming.

The winter of 1939 to 1940 turned into one of the coldest in many years in Holland. Frost often appeared on windows and on the interior walls of houses. Rumours about a German invasion of Holland were flying about, and it was a nervous time for all. Meanwhile, the Nazis pressed the Alsace region of eastern France (where many German speaking peoples resided) on the German border to control the supply of iron ore and coal to feed their war machine. Hitler's intentions were becoming all rather clear now, even to the sceptics. Of course, the Dutch continued in vain to hope desperately that their neutrality would be recognized and honoured and, in fact, the Germans had promised to respect it. Though Holland had been neutral for over one hundred and twenty-five years, including during World War I, that cultural tradition was now on the cusp of disintegration.

Within Inge's family things were quite tight throughout 1939. Aart could not earn enough money as a tailor for daily living expenses for his own family and they relied, to some degree, on grandmother Ingetje's financial support. Inge's mother, Adriana Elizabeth, complained quite a bit and that made the atmosphere even worse between her and Aart. They never knew what Aart was up to at work. In retrospect, Inge observes that a grown man relying for financial support upon his mother-in-law ground away at Aart's self confidence in an era when husbands were predominantly the household breadwinners. Soon after the war Inge's parents would split up. As it turned out, Aart had been seeing someone else during the war and everyone knew it then – except Inge and her sisters.

In Peter's family, Elizabeth had her hands full controlling her brood. Piet and Peter were not doing too well in high school, as too many exciting things were happening! It was feared Britain might decide to invade Holland to establish a beachhead against Germany. But that was just Nazi propaganda. At that time, the British did not really have any significant military capability and the Germans (and the Americans) knew it. Peter says that you could feel the tension rise in the early part of 1940. Germany had conquered Norway and Denmark in April 1940, and Hitler stationed *Luftwaffe* air bases to control that region and others. Next, he wanted to control Holland, Belgium, Luxemburg, France and England, the so-called "Low Countries." After the war, Peter heard that German agents disguised as tourists or students had stolen official police, postal and railway uniforms to pave the way for invading Holland in May that year. This was the Fifth Column or clandestine pre-invasion force designed to grease the wheels for *Blitzkrieg*. The Nazis used that tactic in other countries they targeted too, including England.

Chapter Two

Invasion

Though Holland did everything possible to make its neutrality clear to the world, on Friday May 10, 1940, in the early morning hours Peter and his family were awakened by the sudden sounds of explosions and the noise of a sky filled with planes. A few archaic anti-aircraft flak guns were blazing with little effect; they may as well have been pea shooters, for the Dutch were not prepared for a modern invasion. German paratroopers dropped by the hundreds from the sky above and they came in covert ways too. For example, Peter heard that hundreds of German soldiers secretly lay below the decks of three hundred-foot-long barges docked at Rotterdam harbour near the bridges. The barges had been filled with troops in Germany and then towed down river to Rotterdam as regular cargo. When hostilities began, troops suddenly emerged to set up positions near the bridges. Meanwhile, Peter saw huge sea planes fly low overhead and land on the Maas River unloading equipment and men for their onslaught against the Dutch Marines who were scrambling to set up defensive positions. With all this military might, Hitler's armies barged into Holland without warning using lies about Allied invasions of Germany's Ruhr valley (the industrial heartland of western Germany where there was heavy concentration of factories producing munitions and components to feed the Nazi war appetite) and Dutch abrogation of neutrality as a false pretext to do so. Hitler wanted Holland to come willingly under German rule but most of the population would not oblige him. That said, thousands of misguided Dutchmen either were or became traitorous collaborators and members of the Dutch Nazi party who allied themselves with the German wartime administration.

Peter's bedroom was on the top floor of their four-story apartment building with a flat roof which they accessed from their balcony using a steel ladder. He saw darkish grey coloured Nazi transport planes flying overhead and fighters darting about. Looking on with great interest he heard things hitting their roof and the tile roofs nearby. Peter was lucky not to have been hit by the shrapnel from the exploding flak gun grenades that were firing everywhere. This was the day the war started for the Netherlands. The country had not been in a war since Napoleon withdrew French troops from Dutch soil in 1813, thereby paving the way for the return of the Dutch monarchy.

With the help of an uncle, Peter's family, without Jacob, trekked as refugees to the northern suburbs of Rotterdam where they thought they would be safe from the bombs. Later that morning Peter went to high school as usual. The principal, Mr. Reitsma, stood at the top of the stairs facing the main entry. He informed the students of the obvious and told the boys to go back home to await further developments. However, due to an adventurous spirit, Peter did not take that advice. Instead, he and a couple of friends decided to go and look at the action. Fighting was going on at the Maas River Bridge, a railroad bridge across the Rhine River and at a half constructed tunnel under the river. The bridges were actually no more than a half hour walk from his school and off they went. Below is a photograph of those two bridges taken prior to the war.[i]

Maas River Bridges

The bridge on the left was for pedestrian and public transit traffic and the one on the right for the railroad. Peter and his friends perched to watch the fighting a few blocks away in the foreground of the picture above. The Dutch Marines were fighting the German invaders and were protecting the bridges and the tunnel from the Germans on the opposite side. Peter and his friends got too close to the action and saw pieces of masonry and stone flying off the facades of some nearby buildings under the splitting impact of large calibre bullets. As fourteen-year-olds they were impressed, but they also suddenly realized this was a very dangerous place to be. They soon decided they better get the hell out of there and go home where they spent the next several days waiting and wondering what would happen next.

On the first day of the war Inge and her family fled their home to the countryside about one kilometre away. There, without a tent and with only some blankets, they slept on the grass under the open sky. There were other people in the field too. Inge was very scared at what was happening all around her while battles were being waged. The next day Inge's family moved back to their home to await the outcome, fearful and terrified by the invasion, and the bombings from which there could be little escape. Like so many Dutch city residents in these circumstances, choices for finding true safety were limited.

In response to the invasion, on that first day while his son watched the action near the harbour, Jacob engaged his troops and marched towards Valkenburg Airfield near Leiden (famous for the Leiden Jar where the battery was first invented), Katwijk and The Hague along the North Sea Coast. Rumour had it that German paratroopers had been dropped there. His company of soldiers were equipped with weapons dating from the nineteenth century and with old and inadequate munitions because modern military equipment had not been a priority for a neutral country. There were no Dutch air planes on the airfield, but German ones were attempting to land. Jacob's riveting account of the battle is summarized here.

By the time Jacob arrived at the airfield on that first day of the war nearly three hundred Dutch soldiers lay dead or wounded. As his company approached, German batteries fired on them with machine gun blasts; that "tick tick" sound was heard all around them. When his company then approached the entrance road to the airfield, large transport planes loomed into view. With small arms fire aimed a plane length or two ahead they brought down a plane which crashed creating a massive explosion, boosting troop morale tenfold---they could beat these bastards! But, as Jacob's company pressed on past the entrance road, German fighter aircraft strafed them. Bullets from one of the fighters took out their large calibre machine gun magazine rendering it useless. Automatic machine gun fire from emplacements within the airfield near a "pile driver" was trying to take them out, but they managed to escape serious injuries up to that point.

As ditches and canals ringed the airfield, there were many places for troops to take cover. German soldiers yelled at Dutch troops to give up but Jacob's troops would not comply even though pinned down for a time. In all the commotion, Jacob leapt into a fox hole but, in the middle of his leap, a rifle emerged in front of him. Before he could arrest his speed the point of a bayonet entered his thigh and stopped at the bone. The weapon belonged to a recruit who was busily digging with the butt of his rifle across his shoulder. Jacob steeled himself against the agony.

As this was happening, Dutch mortars blasted landed German aircraft with great accuracy and, like the plane they shot down, those successes bolstered troop morale. But fighters were scouting out the launch and fire locations of the mortar batteries making the situation quite tense. In his battle memoir, Jacob wrote that at one point during the battle when his troops were re-approaching that pile driver behind which lay the machine gun battery:

> That is when the real drama starts.
>
> Unexpectedly comes an enemy burst of fire from the direction of the viaduct across the Wassenaarse Weg, about 600 meters away. The bundle cuts across the entire length of the ditch. Although the men are 4 meters apart, that does not make any difference now.
>
> First the bundle hits Corporal Van Veen, then 2 soldiers, then the Section Commander, Sergeant Scholten, and finally the rear guard Corporal Huygen. Except for the rear guard who is shot through both legs; all of them are killed immediately. One of our own recruits, only a few weeks from the Depot (a boy 19 years old), and I, are the only survivors.
>
> When much later, a few weeks after the war, I return to thoroughly examine what happened, it turns out that a very faint rise in the ground level was the reason why we just missed being seen from the viaduct.
>
> The recruit has an attack of anxiety and crawls halfway under me. He holds on to me with such force that at first that I cannot get away. More through the ground than across it we manage to cross the dam. To free myself I have no choice but to hit the recruit with my revolver. The poor boy keeps crying and after

much persuasion I finally succeed in getting him to come along. War is no child's play.

Jacob's company eventually located that machine gun near the Wassenaarse Weg and fired upon it. In the meantime the Germans continued to fire back at them, and their shooting was accurate. When Jacob raised his helmet with his dagger to determine where the firing was coming from, shots rang out and pierced it. That was about as simple a form of intelligence gathering as one could imagine. Jacob kept that helmet after the war along with his vivid memories of that battle. Below is a picture of the helmet, likely made in the nineteenth century, showing the hole created by the machine gun burst. It remains with our family as a memento and reminder of his sacrifice, and those of other fellow servicemen, who perished in brave defence of Holland in those early days of the war on Dutch soil.

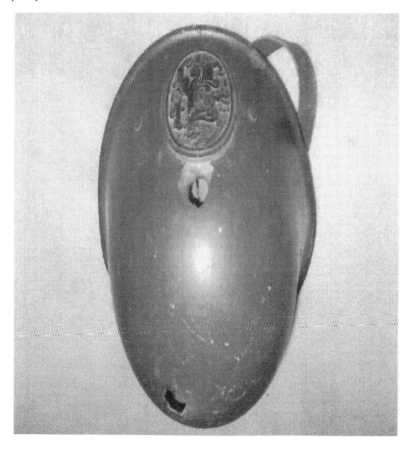

Jacob's WW II Helmet

When Jacob's section got near German planes close to the hangars on the airfield he climbed into several of them and destroyed their dash boards with the butt of his rifle to make sure they could not be used. By this point his leg was hurting badly but he kept on going until he entered a nearby barracks where he came upon a paratrooper. He wrote:

> Quicker than I can describe it here I draw my pistol but the German raises his hands and pitifully smiles at me saying "Ich bin Arzt!" Here I almost shot a doctor to death.

> Now I see the results of the attack. A whole barrack full of Dutch and German wounded. Near the Captain I even find a minister, also in the uniform of a paratrooper. Typical German thoroughness.

Shortly thereafter Jacob came under friendly fire from Dutch soldiers trying to take the airfield that was already taken. Just as that misunderstanding was cleared up aircraft bombs hit the ground and the soldiers dove for cover into existing bomb craters. English planes, whose pilots apparently thought the men on the ground were Germans, were bombing them despite the raising of the Dutch flag.

Jacob eventually made it back to an infirmary where he was patched up and then returned to battle. On his way back to the front he was confronted by Dutch patrols who demanded passwords of which he was not aware. When he got back his company was in its old location near the entrance to the airfield and he had a sigh of relief, "I sag down into my old familiar foxhole. I am 'home' again." That just about says it all; he was in his element thinking about nothing but military life, his comfort zone was there and nowhere else and certainly not with his young family.

On May 12, 1940, Easter Sunday, the Germans were firing on the village of Valkenburg and, within a very short time, flames rose from the roofs of houses. In the meantime Jacob suffered an attack of fever and needed to get a doctor to look at his leg. Permission to go to Katwijk was granted immediately and a member of his Company went with him. He wrote:

> In the dusk we depart. In the neighbourhood of the water tower we are accosted by a double guard post. Our password is not acceptable and we have to meet with the Commander with our hands raised. From the Commander we hear that the password has been changed an hour ago. After he gives us the new one we once again get stopped 100 meters further. Here they don't know anything about a new password and want to

hear the old one. This nonsense with passwords caused the loss of life of one Officer of the 4th Regiment. In reply to a guard's question: "Password?" he hesitated; "The old or the new one"? That hesitation condemned him. The guard shot him to death!

There were other moments of truth too. One is particularly dramatic and occurred while he was subsequently involved in an attack on the Pan. He wrote:

Then comes the most poignant moment of those war days. A mother with 5 children walks in the middle of the road. The eldest cannot have been more than 7 years old. In the carriage is a baby of 2 months old, and 2 others are held by a grandmother. Since Friday morning they have not dared leave their home but now that bullets whistle through their windows they cannot keep it up any longer. Since we cannot take them with us through the dunes we advise them to stay in the middle of the road and stay close to each other. They follow this advice and in this fashion reach Katwijk without any harm, right through "No man's land."

It was not long thereafter as the last hours of this battle neared that evidence of the bombing of Rotterdam would be brought home. He wrote:

At the left side of The Hague, in the direction of the airfield "Iepenburg", a curious glow is visible in the night sky. First nobody pays much attention but as the glow grows stronger we wonder what exactly it is. Where one of us believes it to be the gas tanks at Iepenburg, someone else feels the fire is too large for that. The source must be a lot further in any case. It is probably the petroleum harbour of Pernis near Rotterdam that must have been put to fire. Those of us who come from Rotterdam and Schiedam praise themselves lucky they live far away from that harbour.

In the morning the glow changes into a white column of clouds, while the sky next to it shows a turquoise blue colour. A terrifying sight.

Later on, approaching the afternoon, just as all officers are discussing various matters at the Command post of the Major, a shot falls. It is clear it has come a long distance. Instead of the normal "ticking" it chirps. According to the map the distance must have been at least 1500 meters. It comes from the direction of Valkenburg and buries itself into the ground next to the Major. Immediately a second shot chirps by. At the first shot everybody jumps into the foxholes. At the second shot I find myself together with Captain Segaar and Lieutenant Brouwer in a small stretch of trench. All soldiers have disappeared magically. Taking cover is an art we learned quite well. After a few shots hell breaks loose. Several German machine guns spray a great number of bullets at the Command post. It is very evident that they have come a long distance. Not only do the shots chirp, but they are coming down in descending path, such that it appears the bullets are raining in angle. Although we push our knees against our chins, the bullets make little holes in the sand just a few centimetres above our toes. It seems the enemy has gone hog-wild spending ammunition.

I pick this memorable moment to exclaim: "I don't think I feel like it anymore." It is clear our nerves have been affected. All three of us break out in laughter. Next to me I hear someone say; "Can you believe it; he does not feel like it anymore" Lieutenant Brouwer cannot stop himself from telling the Captain; "You better watch it, he may be looking for another job."

When the enemy doubles its fire, to the point where the branches and leaves rain on our helmets and sand blows everywhere, laughter becomes hysteric. After the double barrage is over, we turn very maudlin. Yet the remark "hog-wild" stays in our mind. It only means the enemy is spending all his ammunition because he plans to surrender. That thought cheers us up again. Later on, in discussions with prisoners, we heard that indeed the Germans were already busy affixing white pieces of cloth to long sticks.

And then shortly thereafter it happened: news of the surrender came. He wrote:

For a second everything is deadly quiet. Then all of us have a feeling of deep, intense shame; that we could not keep it up for even 5 days. Everybody has in their eyes, tears that track through the dirt on their faces. Some break out crying...

Then a rain of rifles, bayonets, pistols, daggers and even ticks from the drummer falls into the foxhole, on top of the pistol of the Major. It is as if, together with our weapons, we are the honour of our people.

Those men of "Brave Disobedience", "No Men and No Money", Beautiful Mutiny on the Seven Provinces", "Church and Peace" have reached their goal. We have now experienced "One-sided Disarmament", and "Broken Rifles".

And, so, for Jacob and his family, occupation and increasing hardship would follow Holland's surrender just as it would for many others.

Chapter Three

Occupation

While Jacob fought the Germans Elizabeth, naturally, was beside herself with worry. The Dutch, armed as they were with weapons from the previous century, did not have a hope against the *Blitzkrieg* – despite valiant local fighting by Dutch soldiers. After nearly five days of war Hitler decided enough was enough and ordered the Luftwaffe to bomb the city of Rotterdam to smithereens killing many civilians and Dutch soldiers and wounding many more. On the following pages are a series of postcard pictures of the aftermath of destruction to Rotterdam that Hitler's bombs wrought in 1940 which Jacob acquired at the time though it is unknown from whom or where.[ii] The first image immediately below is the destroyed *Hofplein* railroad station used by daily commuters.

German high explosive and incendiary bombs flattened parts of Rotterdam which created that evening glow (the firestorm) and white cloud Jacob wrote about in his account of the Valkenburg Airfield battle. Peter's family lived just outside the city centre and their block did not get hit. The reality is that Holland was ready to surrender---and the Germans knew it. However, in their typical "bull in a china shop" way the Germans bombed the hell out of Rotterdam anyway. With their fate upon them, the Dutch capitulated. Queen Wilhelmina and her government fled to England just before the Nazis took power, and set up in exile in London.

With the Nazis now in charge, images of Nazism began to pervade Dutch city life. Swastikas appeared on government buildings and Nazi flags were all around. Wherever German forces were stationed or there were occupation government offices Hitler's picture was always prominently displayed to idolize him. Nazi party officials and military personnel who infiltrated government institutions wanted to absorb Holland into the Third Reich. But, to keep things calm, the Nazis needed people to go about their daily lives in as normal a way as might be possible. Most Dutch hated the Germans for disregarding Holland's neutrality and bombing Rotterdam, though tens of thousands did not. They were the Dutch Nazis; the collaborators and minions who helped

Hofplein Railroad Station in east Rotterdam, destroyed

Laurenskerk Cathedral's thick stone walls withstood the bombardment

Witness to Nazi destruction of Rotterdam

Maas Railroad Station - gutted

Destroyed raised railway network

More destroyed railways

Destroyed harbour area

Rotterdam in smoke and flames

implement Nazi policy and rule in Holland in the hope they could run the show there. The Dutch Nazi Party (*Nationaal-Socialistische Beweging der Nederlanden*, also known as the Dutch National Socialist Movement), led by Anton Mussert, also started to throw its weight around by causing small riots here and there in Rotterdam and elsewhere and acting provocatively to draw out the underground or persons opposed to the occupation regime. That group bought into Hitler's policies lock, stock and barrel. Many of its members would pay the price in due course at the end of the war---and justifiably so. But much of their unforgiveable activity would be forgotten too easily not long after the war ended

Later, in May, the Belgian army surrendered to Germany and the dominoes started to fall. In June it was France's turn when Germany threatened to bomb Paris and Hitler sent his divisions into Normandy (Dunquerque) and around the north part of the Maginot Line – remember Peter's family had breached that line too, on a family holiday! The triumphant German army (*Wehrmacht*) marched under the Arc de Triomphe in Paris while the *Luftwaffe* strafed French civilians fleeing Paris. Hitler's Axis partner, Italy, under Mussolini, then invaded France from the south, but Hitler had done most of the work by then. An armistice between France and Germany was signed in June, 1940 to create the collaborationist Vichy government. Only the British, Canadians and, ultimately, the Americans, could save Holland now.

The German occupation authorities in Holland under the leadership of the Austrian, Arthur Seyss-Inquart, who was prominent in helping Hitler to absorb Austria into the Reich in 1938, said the Dutch did not understand what Hitler was trying to do. By the summer of 1940, as a gesture of goodwill towards his fellow Aryans (Dutch is a derivative of Deustch as in "Deutschland" or Germany and the Dutch shared some cultural identity with Germans), Hitler allowed all Dutch prisoners of war to return home, including, of course, Jacob. Unfortunately, but not unusual for him, he never spoke to his family about his imprisonment---never.

For Peter the impact of the "new normal" under Nazi rule was drastic. His school year ending in 1940 became a loss. He failed grade nine and his brother Piet failed his school year too. The war had intervened; they could not concentrate, could not block it out and carry on normally as the Nazis wanted. Life had changed. German soldiers were everywhere and German occupation troops were paid in Dutch guilders and promptly began emptying stores. Peter went back to school in September 1940 and recalls that the following winter was, again, an unusually cold one for Holland. That winter Peter was able to do some skating on the canals---a fleeting moment of pleasure for there was no pleasure in being occupied by the Nazis---whether German or Dutch Nazis, they were all sadistic bastards just the same.

By radio and newspaper the Dutch military under their German managers ordered all Dutch citizens to deliver their radios to central locations or face the threat of severe punishment of either jail or concentration camp. The authorities did not want them to listen to Radio London or to news from London, where the Dutch government and Queen had fled, but needless to say, plenty of radios disappeared into hiding spots, including one by Jacob in his apartment attic. Everything was now rationed, and obtaining coupons from the food distribution arm of the occupation government for milk, bread or potatoes was important. Gradually, shortages of those basic food items became increasingly apparent. To add to the misery that hunger and disorganization create, occasionally, the Allies bombed Rotterdam as it was an important harbour at the mouth of the Rhine River at the North Sea. When the air raid sirens blared city residents did not know what was happening until after the bombs had been dropped---then it was simply too late for people caught in the friendly fire. Understandably, apprehension ran high among the city's residents.

That year Peter's family moved back to the northern Rotterdam suburb of Schiebroek where they were further away from the harbour, as presumably this would be a safer location. Their home was a two-story townhouse with three bedrooms and one bathroom on the second floor and an unfinished attic. The floor was exposed planks and the ceiling was but the underside of the roof sheathing. His little sister, Truus, got a small bedroom on the second floor while the four boys slept in the uninsulated attic where, luckily, they had enough blankets. A large dormer provided light for studying, but it was never sufficient.

Jan and Jaap, who by then were eleven, went to a nearby public school. For Piet and Peter going to high school meant a combination of walking and street car that took at least an hour each way, longer if the weather was bad, and it rained a lot that year. Elizabeth had quite a job managing the war ration coupons for the family. She prepared their school lunch which was nothing more than a few slices of hard bread with a scrape of margarine or imitation jam or a slice of *koek*, a kind of cake made with molasses. Peter suspected that a good percentage of the content of the bread was sawdust. Sometimes, when Jacob was home, he would ask his kids, "How many slices of bread would you like?" If they picked a large number he would take out his sharp knife and cut the thinnest of slices, almost wafers, and then in that way tease them about all the many slices they could have giving the illusion of plenty. It was bit of a cruel joke. Lousy as his lunch usually was, by 10:00 or 11:00 a.m. Peter had finished whatever he had been given and was hungry until he got home by about 5.30 p.m. Even then there still wasn't much food to eat for dinner. Remember what his mother Elizabeth had said when he was much younger: "Some day you will want." It came to pass, but it would get much worse than a meagre lunch.

In 1941, Jacob had joined the armed resistance of the Dutch *ondergrondse* (underground). He occasionally disappeared from the family, but that was nothing new, he did that before the war too, though at least they would generally know where he was then. I cannot say how effective Jacob's *ondergrondse* activities were or what he specifically did because, curiously, he never discussed it with Peter (or any of his other sons) during or after the war. Peter did not know, for example, that in the small veranda located at the back of the top floor of their townhouse Jacob kept hand grenades hidden there. After the war Inge found out about Jacob's weapons stash from Peter's sister, Truus, whom she would eventually come to know as a friend when she met Peter. Had those weapons been found the repercussions for Jacob, and perhaps for his family, would have been severe; quite likely the whole family would have been separated and shipped to one or more concentration camps. But some chances need to be taken for wartime survival and to oppose hostile invaders when the former government has ceased to exist. There is an old Rotterdam motto that states, *"Sterker door strijd"* (stronger through struggle), and this was apt for both the *ondergrondse* forces and residents in the city at the time.

Meanwhile, strange things were happening elsewhere. German radio reported that, unknown to Hitler, Rudolph Hess (one of Hitler's henchmen) had parachuted into Scotland to make a peace offering to the English. Hitler denounced Hess, and the English put him in prison until the end of the war after which he was sent to Nuremburg and lived out his life in Spandau prison. In 1941, and in breach of their non-aggression pact, Hitler also attacked Russia. That stupid military move, repeating Napoleon's failed military strategy, greatly sapped his war machine. Hitler, like Napoleon, would soon realize he had underestimated the opposition, which consisted of Russian resilience, Russian winter weather and sheer geographic expanse.

During the occupation, the difficulty of life for Peter and his siblings was compounded by their parents' strict religious environment---the war had changed nothing in this respect. They were expected to go to church to have the fear of the Lord imprinted into their being. However, that year Peter recalls the creation of a splinter group within his church because two preachers apparently had a difference of opinion about the meaning of a bible verse. That, of course, was a significant event for the congregation, but simply underscored Peter's general scepticism about his parents' religious devotion and their principles which supposedly pillared their family's life. For Peter's parents it did not change the constraints they applied to the kids at home: they were still not allowed to play outside on Sundays, ride a bike (though they did it anyway), play cards, go to the movies or to the neighbourhood coffee shop. Having fun was supposedly sinful. Peter never had any money to spend anyway. Playing soccer in high school was his only fun other than the interaction with girls there.

The winter of 1941--42 was again very cold and contributed to the dismal way of life plaguing the Dutch of Rotterdam. Generally homes were not insulated, and the only heating in Peter's house was a coal burner in the living room which limited the area heated to that room only. The refrain heard, when somebody left that room, was "close the door!" This was now the third year of exceptionally cold winters. As in the previous two winters, Peter's family like many others, including Inge's, was once again in a battle to stay warm against the creeping cold and to get enough food to eat. In Inge's home there were two coal burners but they used only one of them in the living room because coal was expensive.

Under President Roosevelt the Americans hoped to steer clear of the war; however, as in World War I, their forces came late to the party. The United States did not formally enter the war until shortly after the December 7, 1941, bombing of Pearl Harbour by Japanese naval forces, though they were supplying the British with weaponry before then. By this time the Pentagon, the world's large office complex, was under construction to house the United States war department.[iii] The attack pushed the construction along at breakneck speed.

Holland's exiled government in London declared war on Japan shortly after December 7. My father and his family heard about the progress of the war, including the American declarations of war, on BBC London broadcasts, which they listened to on those radios they kept hidden from the authorities. They also heard about events on German controlled radio and read about them in an illegally printed newspaper, *Het Parool,* and in several other illegal publications disseminated by the underground resistance movement. They did not know when the war would end or if they would survive it.

Food shortages of all kinds, of basic things like bread and milk, were widespread, and rationing became more severe. But the Dutch had to persevere and make do with little food because, like so many others, they had no other choice. Occasionally Uncle Maurits and his wife Tini invited Peter to come for lunch. Maurits worked for the food distribution bureaucracy and had some extra rations. They took pity on that skinny youth and served him some soup and a couple of slices of mealy bread. Peter loved Aunt Tini as she had often spoiled Piet and him before the war. Peter always got a pound of grapes for his birthday and once or twice a year she invited them for a mussel dinner. Now, those were only fond memories for Peter in occupied war-weary Holland. In the meantime, however, Peter tried to focus on his studies in order to keep the prospect of a college or university education on the horizon. That was tough to do on an empty stomach in the midst of the uncertainty about Holland's future if the Nazis were to win the war.

By 1942 it was also becoming increasingly apparent to Peter what Hitler was doing to the Dutch Jewish population. The Jews were forced to identify themselves by wearing yellow stars on their clothing; they were subject to curfews; they were sent to labour camps or were otherwise deported to Poland or Germany. Hitler used the Dutch SS, German police and the Dutch Nazis who proclaimed their loyalty to him to implement this policy. Despite that, the vast majority of Dutch citizens rejected their German occupiers and Nazi supporters and many tried to aid Dutch Jews by hiding and feeding them. However, Hitler's racial policies were gathering steam in Holland too, and there was little except individual clandestine things that the Dutch could do to help the Jews then.

In 1942 Peter met a nice attractive young girl who turned out to live in his neighbourhood---Inge, of course. He always liked fishing. One day while he watched a man fishing in the canal close to his home three girls stopped by to watch too. The three were Inge with her two little sisters, Cor and Roelie. Peter was intrigued by what he saw. A couple of days later Inge showed up at his house to visit with a friend. He had another good look. Inge then became friends with Peter's sister Truus which meant she would come over often. As Peter was only sixteen and Inge fifteen, Jacob and Elizabeth were strongly against their courting out of fear that Inge might affect his studies. This was not the case. He got to know her family, who lived in a ground-floor apartment in a Rotterdam neighbourhood along a *singel*, a kind of canal that is part of the landscaping of the area. The upstairs apartment was still occupied by her grandmother and, as well, a spinster Aunt.

A couple of Inge's uncles on her mother's side were members of the Dutch Nazi party and her cousin, Fritz, was a member of the Hitler Youth while their grandmother, at one time, declared in Peter's presence:"God grant that Germany wins the war." Their family name on her mother's side was Enzlin and their ancestry is German. Inge's family were all very tall people who felt (except her father) that she ought to have chosen a taller friend. Peter never felt very welcome by the Enzlin side of her family.

As a war was raging, the German authorities ordered all street lighting to be blacked out. Further, no residential lights were to be seen on threat of severe punishment for non-compliance. Many orders to turn out lights were posted as notices, first in German and then Dutch, but later in the war in German only. On moonless nights it was absolutely pitch black in the city. Peter was allowed to walk Inge home at night from his place, a distance of perhaps half a kilometre. His absence from home was noticed and timed by his parents, but it was all worthwhile to be with Inge just the same. There was just enough time for him to steal a couple of kisses---*Alstublieft*! (Please!).

By February 1943, Hitler was finally learning his costly lesson about Russia, just as Napoleon had in 1812. The *Wehrmacht*, supported by the *Luftwaffe*, had advanced over twelve hundred miles across Russian and Ukrainian terrain to the important industrial city of Stalingrad pushing Stalin's Red Army farther and farther back into its own territory. Millions of men on both sides of the eastern front were engaged in the advance and ensuing battles. The destruction that German forces rained down on towns, villages and cities and the people within them stuns the mind. Hundreds of thousands of people lost their lives in military confrontations and in arbitrary wipe-outs of pockets of humanity that unfolded across a vast landscape of death. But the manner in which the Germans dealt with those vanquished peoples emboldened the Russians who ultimately defeated the Germans at Stalingrad. After their military debacle, the *Wehrmacht* began its long, slow road of defeat back to Germany. When the Red Army finally reached Germany they unleashed their vengeance on the German population. It would be a classic case of "do unto others as they have done unto you"---or worse. And so it went, but the Germans were not giving up just yet.

Also in 1943, Hitler's forces were starting to tighten the noose more and more on Holland. My father's high school was requisitioned by the German military, and his classes were now held at two different locations---one at the western edge of Rotterdam very close to the house where he was born and the other not far away. The Germans had also conscripted Dutch men between the ages of eighteen and forty-five to work in German war industry factories and labour camps. This was the *Arbeitseinsatz* or forced labour deployment.

Meanwhile, the harbour areas were occasionally bombed by the Allies, and Peter's school was not far away. His grandparents lived in an apartment even closer to the harbour. On March 1, 1943, while Peter was in class, the air raid sirens blared out their crescendo-like warnings about a possible attack that was expected, as usual, to be on Rotterdam harbour. Suddenly tremendous ear splitting explosions erupted as bombs burst on impact. As ordered by their teacher, Peter and his classmates dove under their desks and were worried and scared wondering what was coming next. Clouds of smoke were visible from the windows and rumours and questions started to fly about. Were the Allies invading them? Will the school be hit by a stray bomb? Would the Germans retaliate on the citizens?

What happened was an example of carpet-bombing by the Allied Air Force from a great height with the harbour as the target. That meant all planes dropped their bombs simultaneously over a given area potentially leaving wide swaths of destroyed non-military targets. In fact, on that occasion, the bombers missed the harbour by about a kilometre and destroyed a residential neighbourhood that included Peter's grandparents' home. Luckily they were out that time, but lost all their possessions; other residents were not so lucky.

Over the course of the war the harbour and surrounding areas were carpet-bombed at least a dozen times. When an attack happened the noisy thunderous effects of the explosions drew all eyes and ears towards the harbour area to witness the aftermath of destruction, fires and plumes of smoke rising up and drifting away with the wind. Occasionally, Peter recalls looking in the western sky where a great shadowy dark mass crept closer and closer to Rotterdam; then he knew another aerial bombardment of Germany was getting underway with a possible bombing run on Rotterdam. It sometimes took more than an hour for the one to two thousand bombers to pass over in groups of fifty to seventy five on their way to Germany.

In the summer of 1943, through his underground contacts, Jacob had arranged to send Peter and Piet by steam train to work on separate farms in Hoedekenskerke in Zeeuws-Vlaanderen about eighty kilometres away where he hoped they would get enough to eat. The journey to the farm was treacherous as it meant getting through a couple of police checkpoints along the way. They did not have any papers or money, and the inspection was done by Dutch police under German command. The old black coal-fired steam engine pulled several wagons behind it; the wagon immediately behind the engine was accessible on either side. Two police officers of the *Marechaussee* (the Dutch national police) entered the wagon on one side to check passengers' papers. After they entered, the brothers exited at the back of the train and peered into the passenger wagons to watch the progress of the police. By the time the police were about half way through checking papers, the boys snuck back into the wagon behind the steam engine. They could easily have been exposed by other passengers but were not. Peter also suspected that these police deliberately overlooked them, a small act of protest against the occupation and their German overseers. Anyhow, that strategy for Piet and him worked at the beginning and end of the summer.

Peter does not remember the name of the farmer he worked for in Hoedekenskerke, but he spent July and August there working as a farm hand on their huge property. He was assigned several jobs including assisting the foreman to store hay in a giant barn. There were no hay bales in those days so loose harvested hay was brought into the barn on horse drawn wagons. It then had to be pitch forked up level by level to the roof of the barn. That certainly was demanding sweaty work but it was fun too. He remembers the natural heat generated by these massive piles of hay they created in the barn. Peter helped harvest the grain with implements pulled by Belgian horses; the kind with the dirty whitish shag draped over their fetlocks. These Belgians were gentle giants. The farmer's wife also had Peter plunge raw milk in a churn into butter that was then skimmed off the top as it separated, and he also helped out in the machine shop doing odd jobs. When work was over for the day he slept in the farmhouse attic on a dusty mattress on the floor. Every morning he got up early to do his chores; it was physically hard labour, but he was fed much better than his city cousins. It was a welcome respite from the dismal existence plaguing most residents of Rotterdam, where he would have to return at the end of the summer, something he was not looking forward to doing except to be with Inge with whom he stayed in touch over the summer while she worked for Unilever as a junior secretary.

The farm was also located under the fly path of the Allied air forces. Peter occasionally observed the vapour trail of thousands of bombers spread out like great white puffy clouds in the west as they passed overhead; hours later the planes would return with some stragglers flying with only two engines at a lower height. The German anti-aircraft guns would go crazy sending up their flak (exploding grenades used to bring down aircraft). When flak exploded high in the sky it created a distant "poof" sound and made a circle of black smoke. The smoke circles would then intermingle with each other just like the rings of a juggler set against the back drop of a pale blue sky. Some of these planes would be brought down resulting in great fiery explosions. Watching those thousands of bombers pass overhead on their missions to punish and press the German invaders on their own soil gave them hope of a Nazi surrender and an earlier end to this devastating war.

When he returned from the farm, Peter went back to school in September 1943 for his last high school year. There was less and less food available for the family, and the quality had greatly deteriorated. Elizabeth often sent the twins with a pot to a communal kitchen to pick up weak tasteless soup using their ration tickets. The bread had mysterious ingredients too. The family ate large carrots usually used as cattle food (by then the Nazis had deported most of Holland's cattle to Germany along with hundreds of thousands of Dutch citizens!). It was a very difficult time for Elizabeth. There just wasn't enough food to feed a family with five teenagers. She had the coupons but what was the point when the article just was not available?

It was also another cold, miserable winter and Peter had a lot of studying to do for his final high school exams in May, 1944. The house was always freezing, there was no heat except a bit in the living room; electricity and water were available only a couple of hours a day. These were not ideal study conditions. But he did have light in his life and it was Inge.

Chapter Four

Enslavement

In May 1944 Peter's final high school exams were held in a ruined bombed out building that had remained standing in the centre of Rotterdam after the *Luftwaffe* air raid four years before on May 14, 1940. The roof was repaired but a couple of large holes in the exterior masonry walls were not closed. The students felt as though they were half outside. Luckily the weather held up, at least for the duration of the exams which Peter completed that month. Finishing high school was usually a milestone to celebrate in a young man's life; however, Peter was about to experience the Nazi wartime version of what that meant instead.

Immediately after writing his exams, eighteen-year-old Peter received a summons by mail to his parents' house that he was drafted into the *Arbeitseinsatz* for forced labour deployment. That meant he would likely end up in Germany as a slave worker in a grimy munitions plant or other dangerous war factory. Nazi slave labour programs were organized in other occupied countries as well to meet Germany's wartime labour requirements which exceeded its supply of domestic labour.

In Holland, the German army also engaged in mass arrests of thousands of men (*razzias*) whom they sent by rail or literally marched to Germany to work as slaves in the Nazi war effort. Following is a photograph of soldiers prowling the streets. They would simply surround an apartment block and go from house to house to forcibly round up men to send to Germany. [iv]

German soldiers on the prowl for Dutch men to work as slaves or
for other sinister reasons

By this point in the war, American and British bombing campaigns
within areas of Germany to where prisoners were transported to work was
in high gear. Bomber Command in England, led by a man named Harris,
whose name and role as commander in chief my father recalls from radio,
was engaged in "area bombing" attacks within Germany designed to crush
German morale and bring the Nazis to their knees. Of course, that meant
deliberately targeting population centres with the consequential terror that
followed.[v]

American bombing campaigns, up to the bombing of Berlin and Dresden
close to the end of the war, were focused on oil and transportation targets,
but collateral damage to civilians and homes was often heavy and inevitable.[vi]
The chance of being blown up by friendly fire at a ball bearing or munitions
factory in the Ruhr Valley or elsewhere in Germany or, if not that, of literally
being worked to death, was high for those conscripted by the *Arbeitseinsatz*.
The German Nazis did not give a damn about the welfare of foreign workers,

and the Dutch Nazis fed Germany's insatiable appetite for human labour by assisting the army to round up their fellow citizens.

Rather than comply with the *Arbeitseinsatz* summons and after talking to his family and Inge, Peter decided to go *onderduiken* (underground) and disappeared to work at a strawberry farm in a village south of Rotterdam called Rhoon. He knew full well he would have to stay out of sight for the duration of the war, however long that might be until the Nazis were defeated---hopefully. Hiding Peter was again arranged by Jacob through his underground connections and, though risky, there was no other choice for him---Inge and his family knew it but it was heartbreaking just the same.

Rhoon was only about twenty kilometres away. Peter took a street car and a small local steam train to get there. Along the way he saw German soldiers and SS officers goose-stepping along in grey uniforms emblazoned with red swastikas and black leather jackboots. That sight left him deeply uneasy. If he were stopped along the way and challenged as to his destination or lack of papers he could have been shot or immediately put on a transport truck to be sent to a concentration camp. But he was not, luck was with him. It was a risk both he and Jacob were prepared to take because the alternative was potentially much worse.

When he arrived at the farm, Peter got acquainted with his hosts and worked as a farm hand doing odd jobs, as he had done in summers past. The farmers fed him well though he did not stay with them at night. Instead, he bunked with a nice young couple who were willing to give him shelter from the authorities. He cannot recall their names. Of course, those people took their chances aiding and abetting people like Peter to avoid the *Arbeitseinsatz*, but it was a small act of triumph over the Germans and they were willing to do so.

A risky thing was for Peter to avoid contact with the many German soldiers around who were put up next door to where he stayed; the owner of that house was forced by the SS to billet soldiers there. As well, twice a day on his way to or from work at the farm, Peter passed by the guards whom, he guessed, assumed that he belonged to the scenery and did not bother him. He kept his head down and walked with purpose; it was nerve wracking just the same to know that at any moment he could be told to stop and produce papers he did not have, answer questions he could not answer and get other people into trouble whom he could then not help.

On June 6, 1944 the Allied D-Day landing commenced along the Normandy beaches of France near Caen in the Calvados country side famous for its apple orchards and spirit of the same name. Allied forces landed at beaches we all know were code-named Utah, Omaha, Gold, Juno and Sword along a lengthy stretch of French coastline. While the armies of liberation forged their beachheads and began moving inland, Peter heard about the progress of the war front by word of mouth in Rhoon. Inge's family did not have any hidden radios so they got their information about the invasion from German controlled newspaper written in Dutch of course. She recalls that the invasion reports were highly coloured in favour of a German "victory" in Normandy.

There is much good and bad that can be said about the effect of the liberation on the local populations of occupied countries. Indiscriminate and inaccurate Allied target bombing resulted in civilian deaths in France as it did wherever the western or eastern war fronts were located. In various parts of Holland, the Dutch had faced that issue too when the Allies dropped their bombs on Dutch cities and towns to crush what they thought were German military targets and collaterally killed civilians. When that happened it engendered in the local peoples a sense of hostility towards the Allies. It was an unfortunate side effect of the war that in breaking the bondage of the many, the liberators inflicted great personal loss and tragedy on others--- perhaps losses even greater than any experienced at the hands of their German occupiers. Liberation was not a cake walk for the liberators or the liberated.

While in Rhoon, there was no way for Peter and Inge to stay in touch, except through third parties, to let each other know things were okay. After a couple months on the farm, in late July, 1944, Peter could not resist the wish to go and see her. He was caught up in the hype, and hope, of the war ending soon. Big mistake! He got back safely to her home following the same route he had taken to get to the farm in Rhoon. Inge did not know that Peter was coming, but he made it to her house and was allowed to stay for the weekend. He slept on a mattress in the attic accessible by a ladder that was hauled up flush to the ceiling.

Suddenly, in the middle of the night at 3:00 a.m., the police arm of the Dutch Nazi Party, the *Land Wacht*, banged on the front door of Inge's house waking everyone up and demanding to be let inside. When Inge and her mother came to the door, the police specifically asked for Peter. At first, the women bravely denied that he was there. A policeman then pointed a gun at Inge's mother and demanded Peter be produced; otherwise, he would shoot her. A teary and frightened Inge left to get Peter and the police followed her. She pulled down the attic ladder, climbed up and awakened him. Inge told a startled Peter that eleven policemen had surrounded her house and that he had better appear immediately. She, naturally, was very emotional and overcome by fear of what lay immediately ahead for them while Peter suppressed his own panic and dread as he tried to comfort Inge. She knew they were harbouring someone trying to avoid an *Arbeitseinsatz* summons and feared that Peter would now be hauled away and that she might never see him again.

Peter barely had time to put his pants on lest the police charge up to the attic. Petrified with fear, step by tentative step, he uneasily descended the wooden ladder to the floor below carrying his shirt and tie, as if walking the plank towards a sea of circling sharks. The men of the green-uniformed *Land Wacht* were there, guns at the ready preparing to arrest him. Their job was to hunt down *onderduikers* like Peter who tried to escape being sent to Germany as slave labour. When he got to the floor below, a policeman started to tie Peter's hands with his necktie, but Inge's mother spoke up and they let him put on a shirt first. As the police specifically had sought Peter, this was an obvious case of betrayal by Dutch Nazis who somehow knew he was at Inge's house. Peter always suspected the Nazis within Inge's family who felt this was a way of getting rid of him because they did not approve of his relationship with Inge. That same night the *Land Wacht* also picked up Jacob, Inge's father, Aart, and a neighbour of Inge's family. They let them go but kept Peter whose journey into hell was about to begin.

Peter was then taken to the city hall (*Raadhuis*) in Schiebroek to be interrogated. There, a Dutch Nazi barked out questions about what Peter and Jacob did, whom they associated with and so on. After being interrogated a second time by the same man using intimidation and threats but no violence, Peter was transported under guard to the main jail at the police station, the *Haagse Veer*, where political prisoners were housed. In retrospect, he realized that knowing nothing about Jacob's underground activities protected him. If they had thought he was lying the consequences would have been severe---and not just for Peter. His whole family would have borne the brunt of a severe reprisal by the Dutch police or the German security forces.

Peter was incarcerated in *Haagse Veer* for several weeks, initially in solitary confinement. His cell was very small and dingy with but a rickety low rise cot to sleep on and a dirty blanket for warmth. The little food provided was again horrible: mealy dark bread and watery soup. He does not know what made the bread that colour; perhaps the manufacturer under German direction used inventive ingredients such as coal dust to stretch production in a time of scarcity. He really did not know what he was ingesting, but what choice was there, go on a hunger strike? Inge and Truus tried to visit him at *Haagse Veer* to bring him clothes but that was not allowed, a great disappointment for them---and him. He was completely isolated from his family and Inge now who was terribly distraught over Peter's fate.

While in *Haagse Veer*, Peter was twice transported by truck to the office of the German Security Services, the *Sicherheits Dienst* or German SD (connected with the Gestapo), who had installed themselves at the *Heemrasadsingel* in Rotterdam West. Peter believed this was part of a building previously occupied by a Jewish family deported from Holland. He, along with five other prisoners, were brought to the *Heemrasadsingel* where the SD occupied the top floor. They were led by armed guards up a stairwell where they waited in silence, one by one, until called in for interrogation. No talking among themselves was permitted. Once again, as with his Dutch Nazi interrogator, the SD wanted to know what Peter and Jacob did, with whom they associated and so on. They threatened to send Peter to the Eastern Front if he did not tell the truth but he convinced them he knew nothing of value. Then he was returned to his cell not knowing, of course, where he would ultimately be sent next but fearing the worst---Germany.

Time passed slowly in solitary confinement, thoughts of whether he would see Inge or his family again, would he end up in Germany; all these things entered his mind. It was the fear of the unknown, of not being able to control his future that tore away at Peter, but he had to remain strong to survive. With other prisoners he saw the sky once a day for twenty minutes---a brief respite from his languishing existence in *Haagse Veer*. He dug deep within in order to keep a level head in unsanitary and frightful conditions. Later, near the end of his few weeks there, an old man of about fifty was put into his cell. Peter does not remember the man's name but recalls he said he had been in Indonesia before the war. The man returned to Holland just before war broke out. His timing was terrible.

Under heavy guard, Peter and his fellow inmates were eventually relocated to a holding camp for *haven politie* (political prisoners) in the attic of a large dusty building of the Harbour Police headquarters to await transportation to a concentration transit camp. German soldiers carried rifles and machine pistols and would not hesitate to shoot prisoners for whatever reason---and with impunity.

While kept at the Harbour Police headquarters Peter observed *Dolle Dinsdag*, Mad Tuesday, September 5, 1944. Prompted by Mussert and other Dutch Nazi Party brass, thousands of Dutch Nazis began to flee towards eastern Holland and Germany---the collaborators feared reprisals if the Allies overran them and they were caught in Holland either by mobs or the underground forces. But it was not just Dutch Nazis who were on the run: German forces, both of the *Wehrmacht* and the murderous *Waffen SS*, pillaged Holland in their retreat from northern France and Belgium where they had suffered major losses in battles with the Allies. Those liberated in the areas from north of the deep sea port of Antwerp in Belgium to Eindhoven in southern Holland were jubilant. Peter and Inge recall that the rumours about liberation for all of Holland were rampant. Dutch underground forces, commanded through Radio Orange by Prince Bernhard, son-in-law of Queen Wilhelmina, were agitating to take over Holland as the Germans retreated.

On September 14, 1944, the day of transport from the Harbour Police Headquarters, a couple of hundred anxious men were herded like cattle onto the wagons of a train. At the first stop about fifteen miles away at the small rural medieval town of Gouda, they stopped to pick up men also imprisoned like Peter. While there, one of the prisoners on the platform tried to make a run for it and promptly got shot just twenty feet in front of Peter who was still on the train. Though he did not see it, Peter heard the cracking sound of the gun firing. Through the window of the train car, he saw the dead man's limp and lifeless body carried off the platform by the Dutch police who did such dirty work for the Germans. His thought of making an escape cooled off right there. This shooting was obviously meant to warn the men on board not to be stupid. German guards would not hesitate to show how much power they had over those whom they helped to enslave.

Shortly after that incident, the prison train left the Gouda station and lumbered along in the dark of night. Peter felt a great sense of trepidation about where they were going and what would happen there. The train then arrived at a station in the town of Amersfoort---their destination for now. The German SS and the German Security Services had a concentration transit camp there known as the *Polizeiliches Durchgangslager Amersfoort,* which had been a Dutch army barracks before the war but was now used to assemble Dutch criminals, Jehovah Witnesses, Jews, black market and underground people who had been picked up. The SS and German police ran the concentration camps which provided another source of slave labour to serve the wartime needs of the Reich.

Following is a 1943 aerial photograph of *Polizeiliches Durchgangslager Amersfoort* taken by a British pilot.[vii] You will notice the relatively small size of this camp into which a thousand men were crowded into the eight or so barracks that housed the prisoners. To this day, the Dutch government continues to find prison records from Kamp Amersfoort and other camps that the Germans kept or otherwise were unable to destroy by war's end.

Kamp Amersfoort from the air, 1943

From the train station, the men were marched for about an hour until they arrived at the camp, an area perhaps three hundred metres square and fenced in about three metres high with barbed wire strung and rolled along the top of the fence. At the four corners of the camp was a guard tower manned by a German soldier with a machine gun at the ready. A wire fence surrounded the low-slung barracks buildings. They contained nothing but cots three high with a filthy horse blanket for prisoners to sleep on and to wrap around themselves against the cold. Peter knew where the fleas and lice came from that plagued him long after his incarceration there.

With much shouting and spurring on with batons or guns, the prisoners were led in small groups into one of the small buildings where they were relieved of all possessions, stripped down and their hair cut off. Then, in another structure where there was a pile of used camp clothing from people who had been sent on to Germany, they were ordered to get dressed. The place was filthy. Men in those circumstances are pigs. The camp latrines were disgusting, just a trough in the floor along the wall about twenty feet long as a urinal with a long row of overflowing toilets. Luckily Peter escaped being a member of the group charged with the task of cleaning up that mess.

Peter had had nothing to eat since the day before at *Haagse Veer* jail. That evening he was finally given something to eat: watery cabbage soup distributed from large containers called *gamellen,* a small piece of grey or black bread and a small piece of sausage. The prisoners received one large spoonful of soup in which, with luck, they could find pieces of potato or cabbage leaves and, rarely, a small piece of unrecognizable meat. Also, as part of the taste, a chemical, salt petre, was added to the soup to kill the men's sexual drive. After he had eaten it Peter found out that food was also supposed to be next morning's breakfast! His mother's warning about "wanting" was coming to haunt him again and would do so for the foreseeable future.

The next morning orders were issued in German for *Appell* (roll call) after the guards had checked that nobody was left in the barracks. If the numbers did not agree, the men had to stand there until the missing person was found, perhaps hiding somewhere. Some thousand men were set up in a block twenty men wide and about fifty deep, surrounded by armed guards and *Capos* ready to strike with a baton if they felt a man was not lined up properly. *Capos* usually were also prisoners basically dressed as Peter was but who wore insignia indicating their role. He watched them strike prisoners with their batons or short wooden sticks to assert their authority and show the guards what a good job they were doing in the hope of gaining some advantage for themselves by way of food or better treatment. Perhaps that was their way of surviving but, in Peter's view, they were collaborators too deserving of sanction, if not retribution, after the war. The prisoners generally also wore something indicating whether they were political, criminal, Jews or black marketeers. Peter was issued a number while at Kamp Amersfoort though he was unable to remember it until he received documents confirming his stay at the camp as noted below. He had often searched his memory for the number but he has some blanks there, as if his subconscious had blotted it out for his own good.

The Kamp Kommandant, Josef Kotalla, an SS Officer, roamed and paced around the perimeter of men with his *Capos* and his large German Shepherd who was urged to bite here and there as Peter witnessed a couple of times. Such a dog is not much more than a domesticated wolf easily inclined to bare its teeth and to violence at the urging of its master. Kotalla was a demon and a cruel man (one of many thousands in the SS and Gestapo) who was, as Peter subsequently learned, mentally defective, having been in and out of institutions in Germany before the war. Peter cannot forget his face---and his dog. Under Kotalla's command, inmates died of disease or by firing squad if they were not otherwise shipped onwards to Germany or elsewhere in Holland to fortify German defensive positions.

But there was something else at Kamp Amersfoort too, something sinister, an evil invention of Kotalla's he called the "Rose Garden." This area was approximately ten feet by twenty feet surrounded by barbed wire where a prisoner was deposited by the *Capos* or guards and ordered to stand upright for twenty-four to forty-eight hours, rain, frost or sunshine. In addition, the guards sometimes made prisoners whom they felt needed to be punished in the Rose Garden walk in circles with the finger of one hand touching the earth as the centre of the circle. When they fell down, which did not take too long, they were severely beaten for not following orders, but if they lived, they did better than those who were shot at the whim of SS guards, the police or by Kotalla's order. On the next page is the Rose Garden."[viii]

The Rose Garden torture grounds

It was during Peter's stay at *Polizeiliches Durchgangslager Amersfoort* that the *Battle of Arnhem*, memorialized in the movie *A Bridge Too Far* based on the famous book by Cornelius Ryan got underway in September, 1944. One clear day, about two weeks into his imprisonment, he looked to a distant eastern sky filled with planes flying rather low perhaps at about 2500 feet including huge gliders being towed. Paratroopers (below) [ix] were dropping from the sky by the thousands.

Paratroopers Peter saw while in Kamp Amersfoort

That day was September 17, 1944 the first day of *Operation Market Garden*, as Peter later learned it was called, that lasted until September 25. Many rumours about what was happening filtered their way into the camp through more "recruits." The prisoners all thought the end of the war was a lot closer. They prayed it was. The prisoners had secret hopes for a quick liberation, but any public display was out of the question and would have been grounds for severe punishment---being shot or sent to the Rose Garden. Dutch citizens who were not incarcerated climbed to their roof tops to witness personally what they thought was the hour of their liberation. Perhaps Audrey Hepburn, one of the world's most famous actresses who resided in Arnhem during the war, was one of those hopeful people.

The objective of the Battle of Arnhem, the largest airborne operation of the war (the Market part of it), was to take control of bridges deep inside Holland over the Lower Rhine and Maas rivers controlled by the Germans. The Lower Rhine ran through Arnhem, and capture and control of the Arnhem Bridge was the Allied objective. Thousands of Allied paratroopers dropped around Arnhem, while their military equipment was brought in by planes and large gliders that landed in fields not far from the city. By this point in the war the *Luftwaffe* had been severely destroyed in Allied bombing raids or in aerial combat and it was not too much of an issue. Thus little, if any, resistance was faced. However, SS troops and tank Panzer Corps positioned within Arnhem relentlessly shelled British positions on the opposite side of the Lower Rhine. The British had also landed on the north side of the river and were fighting German troops and tanks there in pitched building-to-building and hand-to-hand battles. Of course many Arnhem residents died in the cross fire. [x]

Regrettably, the Germans held the Allies back at Arnhem and retained control of the Arnhem Bridge at tremendous cost in lives on both sides of the battle lines. This defeat caused deathly delay in the rest of Holland's liberation that General Eisenhower had said was so near. The loss chipped away at Dutch morale in occupied Holland as the anticipation of liberation faded when news of the defeat got out. The Dutch were crestfallen over this development. The Allies lost at Arnhem because of logistical inadequacies (lack of supplies and equipment), tactical reasons (there were other ways than Arnhem Bridge to cross the Rhine relatively near to Arnhem), and weather conditions, but not because of lack of effort or sacrifice. The British actually held the Arnhem Bridge for a few days. The following month, in October, the Americans blew it up. [xi] Train loads of men continued to be sent away to Germany just the same. My father thought he would be on one those trains.

While he was in Kamp Amersfoort Peter was able to submit a highly censored note to his mother through the Red Cross to let her know where he was. She, in turn, let Inge know what had happened to him. He has little memory of his day-to-day time at the camp; despair was part of it, wanting to forget another. However, he remembers forlornly looking to the pine forest outside the perimeter fence wondering whether he would ever get out of that place. He often thought of what things were like at home and how Inge was faring and whether he would ever see her or his family again.

Due to intensified Allied air attacks on Germany, more anti-aircraft batteries had to be installed. Peter concluded that was the objective of the trenches and mounds of earth being dug around the anti-aircraft artillery pieces in Amersfoort. This called for more slave labour to be moved about occupied Holland and Germany. On September 26, 1944, the day after the end of Operation Market Garden, Peter was called up and simply told to join a group of men. Surrounded by armed guards, they were marched at night to the Amersfoort railroad station. The men ended up on an old passenger train---destination unknown but feared to be Germany, long expected and dreaded.

In September 2009, Peter obtained a sixty-five-year-old record of his enslavement in Amersfoort, verified, as confirmed by the documents pictured on the following pages. Though the document confirms when he left the camp (*entlassen*) and his number, "7168," there is no record of where he was sent.

As the rickety noisy train rumbled along, a fellow inmate pointed out that they were going east; Peter could not observe the train's direction from his place in the crowded compartment. Well aware of some of the stories about German concentration and death camps where tens of thousands died in squalid conditions or were otherwise murdered, he had an extreme fear of his immediate future. Guards were installed on top of the train, which usually moved at very slow speed, in order to shoot anybody who might try to escape as the train rolled along. He saw nothing along the way as it was late evening. All rail travel took place at night to avoid being spotted by roaming allied fighter planes. Escape was in his mind, but how? He kept to himself most of the time.

The train eventually reached the river Ijssel, crossed it and stopped at the rail station in the town of Zwolle. The men were literally kicked off the train and marched to the city theatre, the *Buiten Societeit*, across the square from the railway station. The words "*heraus*" and "*schnell*" were a constant in Peter's ears. All the theatre seats had been removed and a layer of straw laid down. The couple of toilets in the building were totally inadequate for a couple of hundred men. The place stank. The same standard bit of food was eventually brought in: cabbage soup, black or grey bread and sausage. They were then allowed to lie down on the musty, dirty straw and close their eyes, but sleep was elusive, impossible.

Our Ref. Notre Réf. T/D - 2 237 439 Unser Az.	Your Ref. Votre Réf. . . . Ihr Az.	Bad Arolsen 10.9.2009

EXCERPT FROM DOCUMENTS	EXTRAIT DE DOCUMENTS	DOKUMENTEN-AUSZUG
It is hereby certified that the following indications are cited exactly as they are found in the documents in the possession of the International Tracing Service. It is not permitted for the International Tracing Service to change original entries.	Il est certifié par la présente que les indications suivantes sont conformes à celles des documents originaux en possession du Service International de Recherches et ne peuvent en aucun cas être modifiées par celui-ci.	Hiermit wird bestätigt, dass die folgenden Angaben den Unterlagen des internationalen Suchdienstes originalgetreu entnommen sind. Der internationale Suchdienst ist nicht berechtigt, Originaleintragungen zu ändern.

Name Nom Name	VAN KESSEL-/-	First Names Prénoms Vornamen	Cegienas Petrus-/-	Nationality Nationalité Staatsangehörigkeit	Dutch-/-
Date of birth Date de naissance Geburtsdatum	29.10.1925-/-	Place of birth Lieu de naissance Geburtsort	Rotterdam-/-	Religion Religion Religion	reformatory church-/-
Parents' names Noms des parents Namen der Eltern	not indicated-/-			Profession Profession Beruf	"pupil"-/-
Last known residence Dernière adresse connue Zuletzt bekannter Wohnsitz	Raadhuisstr. 20, Schiebroek-/-			Marital status Etat civil Familienstand	single-/-
Arrested on Arrêté le Verhaftet am	not indicated-/-	in à in	not indicated-/-	by par durch	not indicated-/-
Confined Emprisonné Eingeliefert	in Police Transit Camp Amersfoort-/-			Prisoner's No. No de dossier Häftlingsnummer	7168-/-
On Le Am	14th September 1944-/-	coming from venant de von	branch Rotterdam-/-	by par durch	not indicated-/-
Category Catégorie Kategorie	not indicated-/-				
Transferred Transféré Überstellt	on 26th September 1944 (destination not mentioned).-/-				
Further indications indications complémentaires Weitere Angaben	The documents mention in addition: reason of his admission: refusal to work; "Arbeitseinsatz Reich".-/-				
Remarks of the ITS Remarques de l'ITS Bemerkungen des ITS	none-/-				

M. Kesting

G. Wilke
for the archives

Große Allee 5-9 · 34454 Bad Arolsen · Deutschland · Tel. +49 5691 629-0 · Fax +49 5691 629-501 · info@its-arolsen.org · www.its-arolsen.org

Certification of Peter's Kamp Amersfoort records

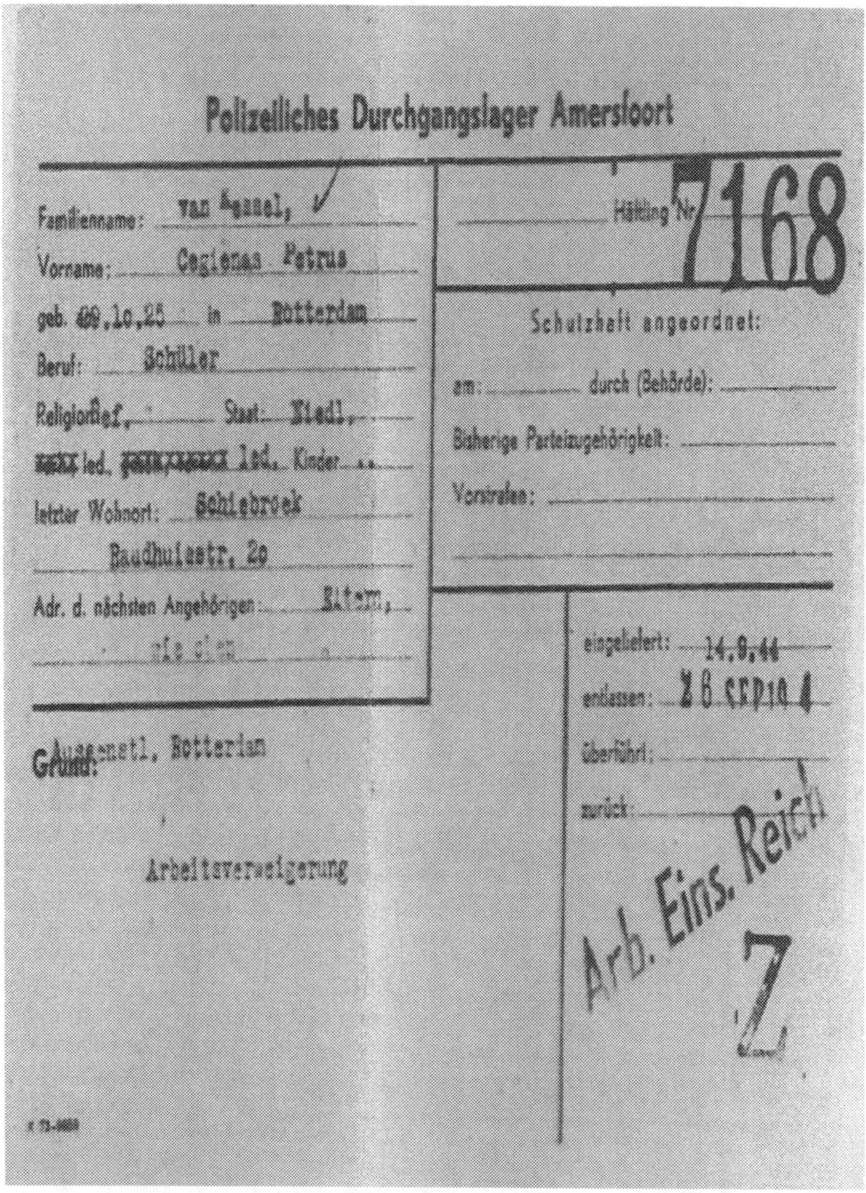

Polizeiliches Durchgangslager Amersfoort

Familienname: van Kessel,

Häftling Nr. 7168

Vorname: Cegienas Petrus

geb. 09.10.25 in Rotterdam

Beruf: Schüler

Religion: Ref., Staat: Niedl.,

led., led., Kinder ..

letzter Wohnort: Schiebroek

Baudhuisstr. 20

Adr. d. nächsten Angehörigen: Eltern, wie oben

Schutzhaft angeordnet:

am: durch (Behörde):

Bisherige Parteizugehörigkeit:

Vorstrafen:

Grund: Aussenstell. Rotterdam

Arbeitsverweigerung

eingeliefert: 14.9.44

entlassen: 28 SEP 1944

überführt:

zurück:

Arb. Eins. Reich

Z

Peter's Kamp Amersfoort entry and exist record

7168.

van K e s e e l C e g i enas Petru;

geb. 29.1o.25 in otterda m

EINGELIEFERT: 14.9.44
ENTLÁSSEN: 6 SEP 19 4
ÚBERFÚHRT: Z

Second page of Peter's Kamp Amersfoort record

The next morning at daybreak with lots of shouting "*Schnell, Schnell*", guards lined the men up in columns of three or four wide and twenty five or thirty deep. Marching the prisoners to work the Germans required only a couple of guards at the rear who occasionally fired their guns to remind the men to stay in line and not be stupid. The guards now were mostly older men between fifty and sixty years of age, whose armed presence alone was enough to keep the prisoners in line. Along the way, local citizens were allowed to hand the prisoners an apple or some slices of bread, but all verbal contact was forbidden.

The prisoners arrived at their place of work on farm land north of Zwolle which was up to two hours marching outside the town. Once at a field they were ordered to dig and build by hand an earth wall around anti-aircraft artillery pieces placed there by the military before they arrived. On other days they were marched to the middle of a *Polder* (embankment or dike) and given shovels to build up more earthen protection for the artillery pieces. Polders in this area were below dikes and part of a flood plain or other area of water that had been drained. It was essentially low land used for cattle grazing or farmland wrested many centuries ago from the sea and surrounded by dikes to prevent flooding. Ever since the days of the Romans, Holland has been reclaiming wetlands by building dikes and polders. Within a polder the Dutch would set up wind mills designed to pump water up several levels until it flowed out into a river or tributary.

When the day was finished and dusk arrived, the prisoners were marched back to the same wretched theatre to lie down on the dirty straw. While in Zwolle Peter once became ill with food poisoning and spent a couple of days in the *krankenlager* (sick bay). This was no more than a room in a lower level of the theatre with straw on the floor. The doctor was a medical student. There was very little discussion with his fellow prisoners in the sick room; Peter was always worried that one of them would turn him in if he spoke of escape; traitors could be anywhere trying to gain favours from their captors. This kind of awful drudgery went on until the end of November 1944. It could have been worse for Peter, he realized, because while in Zwolle, he saw long columns of men coming through that area on their way to slavery in Germany. Following is a photograph of such a line of men.[xii]

Thoughts of Inge and his family were never far from Peter's mind. During these slow and tearful months Inge was loaned out by Unilever to a government company where she typed forms and took shorthand in connection, incredibly, with claims made by people whose homes and other property had been destroyed by either German or Allied bombs during the war. It seemed as though this was a sort of social service authorized by the Nazis to make restitution to their victims; no doubt it was an attempt to manipulate or garner support from the local population for their policies.

Slave march of Dutch men sent to work in Germany

Occasionally allied fighters strafed the anti-aircraft gun emplacements (usually a couple guns were placed close together). When that happened, the prisoners ran away as far away as they could, although they were still under control by the guards, while bullets pasted the flak guns and earthen walls protecting them. On one occasion Peter recalls that during a strafing run by an Allied fighter, one of the prisoners tried to make a run for it. He got perhaps two or three hundred yards away. Peter saw the guards shoot at him but they missed. Then they went after the man, catching him about an hour later. He belonged to the Jehovah Witness, a religion the Germans detested. The Nazis pursued them like the Jews. Peter was not sure at the time if the man would make it, but he thought that his escape attempt had not been a smart move. There were no places to hide in that open country. Perhaps the man was desperate; Peter cannot honestly say that he was not as he, too, was almost at his limit. It sure made him think. This was open country with very few trees around and that fact militated against escape as well as underground activities in such areas. Peter never saw the man again and assumes he was shot.

This period was also when Germany positioned its V-1 and V-2 launch vehicles and rockets in occupied Holland along the coast in The Hague and elsewhere in Holland and Germany to rain down exploding missiles on England or advancing Allied positions. Peter recalls the sound of the V-2s as very loud, specific and not muffled; a rather frightening sound. When the sound stopped he knew the rocket was going to fall down and explode with drastic consequences. The following quote captures it:

> From their homes in Den Haag, residents saw quite a few V2s blast skyward. Watching the tall missiles roar off their firing tables was an awe-inspiring experience for onlookers. But to the launching unit technicians and engineers, preparing a V2 for firing meant hard work and tense nerves. The V2 was such a sophisticated weapon that even the smallest error might cause it to malfunction and crash, or blow up on the ground. Many of the firings took place in the many restricted areas called *"The Sperrgebiet"*. One of these was a three-kilometre strip of land along the coast where all residents had were forced to exit earlier because of construction undertaken for Hitler's *Atlantik Wall*.
>
> Security measures along this strip were strict. The Germans wanted no persons to see how their rockets were prepared and launched, but civilians still managed to get close enough for a good look. Some young children were free to go in and out of the restricted area. They would gather firewood for their families, and could go into the *Sperrgebiet* without being bothered. Once inside the restricted zone, however, some children became acquainted with some of the German soldiers. They would strike up conversations with the uniformed men and found out good information. Some of these children even saw a dangerous V2 launch up close at times....
>
> The residents of Den Haag were still unsuspecting victims of out-of-control rockets. A rocket launched from *Ockenburg* on January 1 came down in a heavily populated area at (17.17 hr.). Several meters above the launch table the rocket turned 160 degrees, then blasting low over two cemeteries, it came down on the houses in the Indigostraat, corner Kamperfoeliesstraat, at a distance of 3600 meters from the launch site. 38 people

lost their lives. The Dutch doctors and nurses, who arrived very quickly, could not start with their work until after the Germans collected the remains of the rocket. [xiii]

One gloomy day as he was working on a flak gun emplacement, Peter looked up and saw his first ever "V" formation of geese flying south, perhaps about fifteen or twenty of the birds. The guards fired their guns but were unable to shoot one down. They swore *scheisse* at the birds passing overhead. Also, almost daily now, the Allied bombers flew by high above and put the German anti-aircraft guns to work, but with little success. Although the shrapnel rained down, nobody was hit to Peter's knowledge. But, for the prisoners, it represented just another way to potentially get killed by being clunked on the head by falling shrapnel.

Peter forgets the exact date, but he believes it was around December 1 when, in the middle of the night, the Germans selected about fifty prisoners (including him) who were marched under armed guard at night to the Zwolle railroad station. They were put on another old-fashioned passenger steam train, each compartment having its own exit door to the platform--- destination they feared Germany. By then Peter knew he was determined to either jump off the train or run away if an opportunity presented itself. He had reached desperation point.

After they boarded, the men discovered the compartment door on the train could be opened and, of course, then the matter of escaping was silently discussed. However, the moment the train started to move Peter realized, to his surprise, it was going west across the river Ijssel and immediately turned south towards Arnhem. That was some relief as by then he was aware of the existence of *Vernichtigungs Lagers* (death camps). Some of the guards warned them that, if caught escaping, that is where they would end up. Any suggestion that the German soldiers or German populace did not know about the death camps is nonsense. Among all the ever-present threats such as being shot, worked to death, illness in unsanitary conditions, being kept behind bars or barbed wire mesh, blown up by friendly Allied fire, being sent to a death camp by the SS for whatever reason was top of the list to be avoided. But when desperation meets reasonable opportunity none of those things seem to matter if you possess the fortitude to bolt.

Around midnight Peter and his fellow prisoners arrived in Arnhem, a city largely destroyed by the battle a few months earlier. The city centre and rail station were in ruins: burnt-out buildings, busted concrete, rubble and garbage were everywhere. This was where the battle had happened three months before when, in Kamp Amersfoort, Peter saw the many bombers and gliders flying low in the far eastern sky.

The men were then lined up to march west to an area about fifteen kilometres away close to the Lower Rhine River and were put up in what had been a senior citizens home in Heelsum to the west of the destroyed Arnhem Bridge. The building had two wings with the centre consisting of a stairway to the second floor with rooms on both sides off a long hallway, not unlike a motel. Each wing had perhaps fifty beds. Individual rooms were about ten square feet. Six men were put in each room on straw a foot deep. It was old, stinking, and freezing cold as they had no heat and no blankets. The Germans had surrounded the place with low-rise barbed wire to box the prisoners in and guards patrolled the perimeter fence. A hunk of bread with a small piece of sausage was going to be that day's ration until the famous cabbage soup in the evening. It was miserable but they ate it all just the same---again, they had no choice.

The prisoners were allowed to freely search deserted homes in that area for any food but not much was found. All homes had been vacated as the Germans expelled the residents to create the *Sperrgebiet*, a strip of land a couple of kilometres wide along the Lower Rhine River on the north side. As in the V-2 citation earlier, that meant that if anybody was caught inside the area, unless they had a special *Ausweis* or pass, they risked being considered as a spy. The penalty for this was being shot on the spot. There were signs around warning the men of the *Sperrgebiet,* and the guards barked out orders and explanations about it.

The prisoners were brought to Arnhem because the Germans needed help to dig trenches to prepare for the next Allied offensive. Though they could not be seen, the Allies were right across the river only a couple of kilometres away as this was now the western front line. Occasionally artillery gunners lobbed shells to the German-controlled side of the river. One wing of the building Peter was housed in, luckily unoccupied, was hit and blown apart. Though the liberators were just a short distance away, there was nothing Peter could do at that moment as his reach for freedom exceeded his grasp---for now.

Chapter Five

Escape

The next couple of weeks were stressful for Peter, caught as he was between the prospects of intermittent Allied artillery barrages and being shipped to Germany. The thought of escape and looking for a chance to get out of there frequently came to his mind. The prisoners were housed in a wooded area where Peter saw lots of evidence of the Arnhem battle: shell casings, unused ammunition, abandoned equipment, the ruins of houses hit by artillery shells, and lots of severely damaged trees. While there, Peter never discussed with anyone his thoughts of escape for the usual reason: traitors could be anywhere. He kept his own counsel.

Then the Battle of the Bulge started in the Belgian Ardennes not too far from where, in innocent times past, Peter and his family had enjoyed summer holidays in the 1930s. He could hear the battle sounds and explosions as a low distant rumble. He also heard German guards discussing the battle, and they confidently told the prisoners they expected to be back in the Belgian port of Antwerp in a few days---not the kind of news the prisoners were happy to hear. In the meantime Allied artillery batteries continued to lob the odd shell into his area, presumably to keep the Nazis awake. Peter then grew increasingly anxious about being hit by one of their shells. Fear and escape consumed his thoughts.

The Battle of the Bulge was Hitler's last-ditch major ground offensive to divide up the Allied forces. It had the effect of creating a "bulge" in the primarily American front lines in the Belgian Ardennes in Houffalize, which my father's family passed through on their holiday in 1935. But the German army had inadequate fuel supplies and bogged down, with the result that soldiers left their tanks and other vehicles and marched back towards Germany's Siegfried Line, also known as the "West Wall." Similar to the Maginot Line of defence, the Siegfried Line was marked by concrete fortifications designed to protect homeland Germany from invasion. But the Siegfried Line was not well defended because Hitler had not devoted resources to it. He always arrogantly thought he had better judgment about what to do about the West Wall than his Prussian Generals, who did not think as highly of his military prowess as he did, to say the least. Many thousands of men lost their lives on both sides in the Battle of the Bulge, which continued through December and January 1945.[xiv]

And then Christmas Day December 25, 1944, came around, a most pivotal day where opportunity met Peter's desperation. He discovered many of the German guards were drunk. Suddenly, he had had enough and did not care anymore; he decided on the spot it was now or never as there was still a strong chance of being dragged back to Germany where the Allies were flattening German cities and towns, or becoming an unintended casualty of an Allied artillery shell if he remained in Heelsum. When he noticed that the army patrol which usually guarded the barbed wire perimeter fence was not there, Peter scrambled over it, scraping and etching the barbs in his hands and legs. On the opposite side of the fence there were trees everywhere, though the forest was not dense. He slipped into the trees that then gave way to scrub land covered with heather. He had not said anything to any of his fellow prisoners; he just ran---fast---and got away! Who knows what patrols could have been lurking out there in the trees? But it just did not matter to him anymore. His escape from Nazi hell had begun.

Peter knew, more or less, where he was and aimed for the west running through forest and fields as fast as he could. In passing through a rather large open area after about one hour, he came upon one of the landing zones near where the Battle of Arnhem had taken place as evidenced by the wrecked gliders lying about as well as other abandoned military equipment and spent ammunition. Like the first morning of the invasion on May 10, 1940, when he and his friends went to see the front line fighting in Rotterdam, curiosity got the best of Peter as he checked out one of the crashed gliders and all the equipment strewn about. Twice he heard bullets whistle past his head as soldiers somewhere had spotted him and were sniping to bring him down. Rushed by instant adrenalin he darted away and fled as fast as he could. The fear of being caught or shot drove him on while he scrambled through woods and open areas. There was no stopping now, and he did not look back. Either he would make it or not, but anything was better than the hopelessness of remaining in captivity.

The town Peter aimed for was Ede, located just outside the *Sperrgebiet*, perhaps five kilometres away. He managed surreptitiously to slip into town in late afternoon. He had not run into anyone before reaching town, but when he got there Ede was crawling with hundreds of German troops, who seemed however to ignore him as they were busy getting ready to go somewhere, probably the front lines. He was careful to avoid eye contact with them. He had to become part of the scenery, so to speak, with which he had some prior experience in Rhoon. A thought came to him that a single man walking the road at that time in the late afternoon in prisoner's clothes risked being ordered to show papers---he did not have any! Had this happened, it would likely have been the end of his escape then and there. Someone was bound eventually to spot him in his prison clothes soon unless he somehow could blend in.

But, as luck would have it, Peter got through the small town of Ede safely and then, on the edge of the other side of town, he saw an older man of about fifty, a younger man, and a boy about twelve pushing a cart with potatoes, other vegetables and some grain along the main road to Utrecht, the *Utrechtse Straatweg*, which was bricked the entire way. He approached the people and asked if they needed help as he would gladly give them a hand. They happily accepted as they were probably tired and hungry. They had been on the road for a couple of days going from farm to farm to beg for food. They were from the city of Utrecht. He caught their names at the time but cannot remember them now. Though they had food they could have eaten from their own cart, they were trying to save it for the folks back home. They were lucky the Germans did not steal it. Peter was lucky they were there. His ruse to avoid detection by the German soldiers worked.

A large number of city people were on the roads with carts or bicycles trying to gather food for their families in the city. Together with this man and his sons they begged for food at the next farm where the farmer there gave each of them two slices of his own bread with some fresh milk, food that Peter had not seen in months. It tasted delicious (most farmers in Holland during the war were never hungry). They slept in a barn there, a luxury compared to anywhere else Peter had slept in the last five months.

The next morning they continued their journey along the *Utrechtse Straatweg* and eventually arrived at the roving peoples' place in Utrecht where Peter was offered not only something to eat but a bed for the night after he had cleaned himself up. He had not had an opportunity to do that for a long time, and a bed as opposed to straw was like floating on air.

Meanwhile Peter had sustained up an eye infection easily picked up in unsanitary conditions, pink eye, as it was called by the eye doctor in Utrecht whom he was fortunate enough to see. It was Nazi policy that all Dutch doctors register as Nazis, but they greatly resisted. The doctor probably was registered but was disloyal as most were, and he was known to the man with the cart. After Peter had been seen by the eye doctor, those kind people gave him one of their bikes to try to travel home the last fifty-odd kilometres, with the request to return it when possible. He thanked them profusely and promised to do his best. It was an old bike but it was functional and held up as he rode it towards Rotterdam.

It was icy cold and foggy and Peter froze as the old and worn prison pants and a jacket were inadequate. He also wore an old hat to keep his head warm - and to fit in. By nightfall after riding about thirty kilometres he had to get off the road somewhere to get some sleep as he was exhausted. Upon seeing a promising farm house in the dusky light Peter went down the lane and knocked on the door. When it opened a uniformed German officer appeared. "*Was wollen sie,*" "what do you want," he demanded in an authoritarian tone. Peter will never forget those ten seconds of terror that seemed to him to last ten hours while he stood there like a stone. That encounter was more gut-wrenching than when he descended the attic ladder in Inge's house and was arrested by the *Land Wacht*. Once again his mouth turned dry from fear just as it had five months earlier when his ordeal began. What would he say, what should he say, would his escape end here and now after all the chances he had taken? Should he run? He couldn't, he felt momentarily paralyzed. If he darted he might be shot by the officer or a patrol might be sent to hunt him down and execute him on the spot.

Then he spoke. Peter told the officer he was on his way home, but it was late and he hoped to find a place to sleep for the night. He could hear the sounds of a party and singing in the background, likely a New Year's celebration. The officer looked sternly at him for a moment and then he replied, "Not here you don't. Go to that place over there as they will most likely be able to accommodate you." The officer pointed that place out to him. Peter said "thank you very much," and the officer shut the door.

With his wobbly legs Peter got onto his bike and rode it back down the lane with a great sigh of relief. He thought that was the end of the line for him---again. But the German officer was telling the truth; the people in the next farmhouse received him well and gave him something to eat and a place to sleep in their attic on an old steel bed with a mattress and a couple of blankets, and for the first time in a very long time he was warm that night. He had been through a Nazi prison nightmare that he was about to wake up from, he hoped. By then Peter was only about twenty kilometres away from home. The farmer warned him that German Army check points were on all roads in and out of Rotterdam, but that he knew some of the soldiers and would help Peter to pass through without being checked for papers as he had none. The troops were looking for the *Ausweis* permits residents needed to be outside or on the road.

It was cold and dark the next day as the farmer and Peter approached the checkpoint, the kind of day when you think something bad is going to happen. The farmer talked to the soldiers and, sure enough, they let him through. Peter does not know what the farmer said to them, but he wished good luck to my father, who rode away on his bike with his spirits raised.

Peter always wondered about this good deed; the man could have been a Dutch Nazi and turned him in, but he was not. He was just a good-hearted soul who had some sway with the soldiers, perhaps he fed them, who knows. Nonetheless, relying on the farmer was a another in a long line of chances that Peter had to take. He never saw the man again; it was almost as if he was a guardian angel. Peter had a few of those along the way.

Once through the check point the coast would be clear to home except for the Dutch Nazis if they were about. Peter continued to ride down the main highway from Utrecht to Rotterdam. There was hardly anybody on the road other than the odd German Army vehicle; nobody paid any attention to him. The Germans, particularly the *Waffen SS*, acted indiscriminately, mercilessly killing Dutch civilians for even the most trifling transgression, as they did everywhere under Nazi occupation. They might have been in any one of those vehicles and stopped to mete out retribution more or less at random. But Peter kept on riding and eventually reached his destination---home---after five months of captivity and many brushes with death.

Entering through the gate at the garden in the back of his home he encountered his younger brother, Jan, who did not recognize him. Jan called him *"Meneer"* (Sir). It was quite a homecoming for both Peter and Jan. His older brother Piet was not there, but Jacob and Elizabeth were, as well as Jaap. Elizabeth received him with open arms. Jacob also welcomed him back but did not speak to him much at all. To Peter, there was something dysfunctional about that. He asked about Inge and was told she was travelling, accompanied by his sister Truus, hoping to find him. He could not believe that the girls' parents had let them go on such a trip. That, of course, was a sharp disappointment to Peter as well as a great concern about what might happen to them. He suggested to Jan that he had a job for a fourteen- year-old and that was to return the bike to the people in Utrecht and to walk the fifty kilometres back home again. Jan returned the borrowed bicycle, and came back home a couple of days later. Peter always appreciated what his little brother did!

It so happened that Inge and Truus returned home safely just before New Year's Eve. She and Peter had a lot to talk about. He told her about the terrible things that had happened to him in the previous five months, but it was Inge's story that gripped him then. She told him that Truus and she had decided to try to see him while he was at Zwolle, as Inge had received a censored note saying he was there. Their adventure took quite awhile to plan, but they decided to go as soon as possible in December. They had arranged to travel by bicycle on whatever bikes they could find in their neighbourhood. And luck was with them, they found two dilapidated little bikes (*fietsen*). As the smaller girl, Truus chose the smaller bike, and off they rode via Utrecht towards Zwolle.

Inge and Truus begged for food at farms along the way. Although they were hungry and needed a bath too, their concern was Peter. They just kept going driven by the hope they would be able to see him soon. They were just two girls travelling on rickety old bikes, on their own, completely out of contact with their families. That they might have been picked up by the police or German soldiers never entered their minds. They arrived in Zwolle only to discover that Peter had been moved to Arnhem, according to some of the Zwolle locals. When they found that out, Truus wanted to travel on to Arnhem (Inge remembers that Truus was a daredevil). They were in a dilemma about what to do next. Inge and Truus argued and argued, but eventually they decided that it was better to go back to Rotterdam as they had no food, two rotten bicycles and there was a chance that they would be picked up on the bridge at the west end of Zwolle on the Ijssel River if they stayed. Luckily, they were not picked up and guessed they were fated to live a little longer. Truus and Inge turned around and travelled back on their bicycles through Utrecht to the home of Truus' future aunt and uncle and slept the night with them in a large bed to stay warm against winter's cold and icy grip.

The next morning they got up early, packed their bikes with a sack of flour for their mothers and something to eat on the road, a simple sandwich for the long trip back to Rotterdam. They rode till they arrived at the centre of Utrecht and then one of the bikes fell apart. They laughed and laughed, as girls might do in such a situation, although there was nothing to laugh about. They just sat on the street and decided that they better walk with one bike by hand. That was hard for Inge to do as she was much too tall for the bike but they walked to Rotterdam nonetheless. There were only a few German vehicles passing on the road, but the drivers did not stop or pay any notice of them. The vivid memory and purpose of that trip never faded from Inge's or Truus' mind.

Unfortunately, Peter had to go underground again but, because of the way the war was going now, Dutch Nazis were lying low and were not expected to be much of a problem anymore. Many of the collaborators had fled to Germany in September 1944 during *Dolles Dinsdag*. All the same, Peter tried to stay out of sight as much as possible, as there were still German soldiers around and traitors could be anywhere. The electricity and water service to homes was shut off most of the time that winter, as Rotterdam did not have the fuel needed to power these services. Food rationing worsened and, even if the family had the required coupons, the food was simply not available. That winter was later called the *Honger Winter*.

Peter and Piet had joined the *Binnenlandse Strijdkrachten* (Dutch underground army) that was being assembled to be ready for the liberation that was now imminent. It was thought that without such an army mob rule and revenge might take place against Nazi collaborators. Of course, that happened in some quarters regardless, and was likely overlooked by some authorities, but perpetual mayhem was not on the political agenda for the Dutch government in exile, and therefore it was important for them to be ready to control possible outbursts of street revenge.

On the next page is a diagram of Peter's five-month journey superimposed in arrows on a map of The Netherlands: it begins with his arrest in Rotterdam, followed by his rail transport to Gouda, Utrecht, Amersfoort, and then his further train trip to Zwolle, Appeldoorn and Arnhem where he escaped; finally, it shows his journey on foot through Ede, Zeist, Utrecht, back through Gouda and, finally, home to Rotterdam and Inge.[xv]

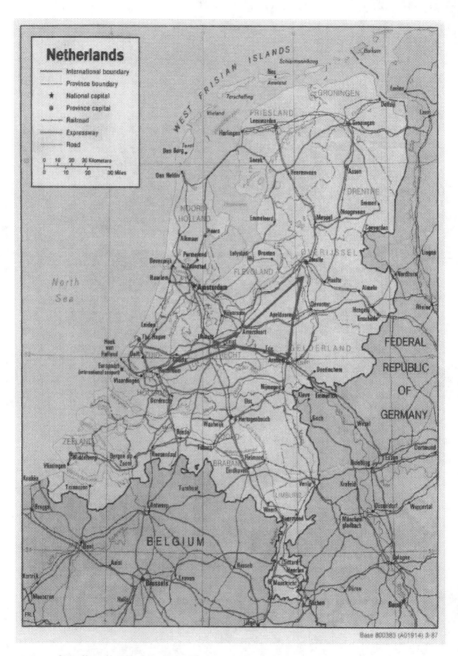

May of Holland with overlay in arrows of Peter's journey home from Arnhem

Chapter Six

Starvation

Peter's successful escape was not the end of his or Inge's difficulties---starvation followed. During the horrible *Honger Winter* of 1945 millions of Dutch remained under Nazi occupation until the bitter end of the war. Children and adults scrounged for scarce food or what might barely qualify as food, while many thousands suffered from malnutrition. Somehow Jacob was able to lay his hands on a few large carrots or sugar beets, anything to put something in the stomach. The field across the canal in front of their house had old sprouts that they picked to eat. They secretly cut down some small trees, chopped them up, and used the wood for fuel. In the city, people resorted to cutting up closet shelves and doors, anything made of wood, including furniture just to have a bit of heat. They were desperate for warmth.

In both Inge and Peter's homes there was black paper on the windows so that light would not show through. Everything was dark in the house, contributing to the pessimistic brooding mood that arose from both the *Honger Winter* and the squeeze of military occupation. Inge was not allowed to be outside during curfew hours, but like many young people, she was not always careful and went outside anyway. First, it was a ten o'clock curfew, then it became six o'clock. For Peter it was basically a twenty-four-hour-a-day curfew, self-imposed for his own safety.

As you can imagine, the nights were long and dark; there was basically no light except for the odd candle. Inge's mother had a carbide lantern and sometimes a candle made from a bit of oil and a wick, which gave a little light and a futile bit of heat. Then there was always the fear. Her mother used to say that Inge could hear the planes take off in England which is why she frequently sat on the stairs at night with clothes for everybody in the event they had to escape quickly. Like everyone, Inge was afraid of the prospect of being unintentionally bombed by the Allies. Some of that fear was still with her even after moving to Canada. Certainly, in dozens of German cities and towns, thousands died horribly in firestorms created by English terror raids when phosphorous incendiaries fell followed by high explosive bombs. The

Allies were not liable to do that intentionally to Rotterdam. But who really knew at the time?

In the unliberated part of Holland, which included Rotterdam, the Germans "pursued a policy of vengeance against citizens of the Netherlands, and deliberately allowed them to starve." [xvi] The point is well illustrated by the following quotation:

> During the later winter and early spring of 1945, when life had revived in liberated Brussels and Paris, northwest Holland was a lifeless zone of darkness and hunger, a pitiful encampment of skeletal children and cadaverous people, surviving on tulip bulbs and beets. The Dutch people's deliverance did not come until the collapse of the Third Reich itself, by which time some 16,000 people had died of starvation in what had been one of the richest, most intensively cultivated countries in Europe...[xvii]

Perhaps because the unliberated part of Holland was not as strategically important to the Allies as their race to Berlin, the Dutch people in the area endured an additional eight months of suffering. But it is too late in the day to cast blame, and my parents are grateful for the extraordinary efforts and sacrifices hundreds of thousands of Allied soldiers made to free the Dutch from Hitler's grasp and the sharp nails of tyranny.

The roots of the mass starvation and malnutrition of the *Honger Winter* may be traced to policies adopted years earlier. Harvested food during the wartime growing seasons as well as livestock had been sent to Germany to feed the Germans, leaving many Dutch severely undernourished by 1945. By the time of the *Honger Winter,* Germany had stripped Holland bare.[xviii] My parents recall that early in the winter of 1945 Sweden tried to help by delivering food supplies to Rotterdam for bread, but it was not nearly enough. Bread was available only in small loaves, and you had to stand in line for it. Inge did not stand in line as often as her sister Cor because she had a sore hip due to a genetic malformation. Caloric deprivation, disease and other problems tore a strip off Dutch morale that only exacerbated the psychological stress already caused by the Allied loss at the Battle of Arnhem and the threat of a German return to Antwerp had the Battle of the Bulge gone the other way. The lack of proper, or any, food prior to liberation was at the core of the Dutch struggle for survival.

When the fighting continued and basically bypassed Rotterdam, my parents realized that liberation was not coming for a while. At this point, the Germans held the population of western half of Holland for ransom. They threatened to open the dikes and flood inhabited places if the Allies tried to conquer the rest of the Netherlands. In fact, they did so in some parts of the country, Wieringermeer and Nijmegen, as Peter recalls. In addition, they set fire to fields and hay stacks. Below is a photograph of the type of tactic employed by the retreating German army at Wieringermeer [xix]

Flood at Wieringermeer polder due to dike destruction

In addition, Peter recalls, in order to leave a mess for the Allies, the Germans mined lengths of Rotterdam's harbour walls by breaking open the pavement next to the wall, drilling holes, placing explosives, and then blowing up the walls to prevent practical use of the docks by incoming ships. Such were Germany's closing acts of retribution to the Dutch for not joining with them.

For Peter, the next few months up to April, 1945 were a battle to stay out of sight as well as to scrounge for food and fuel. It was well known that the German army was still rounding up Dutch men to send as slaves to Germany even at this late stage in the war, in addition to carrying out murders on the streets. The history books are filled with examples of their brutality. Some of them did it just for fun; that is how little esteem they held for human life. German soldiers continued to surround city blocks in Rotterdam and round up thousands of men (*razzias*) who were shipped to Germany by barge or train or marched there on foot.

Peter secretly visited Inge frequently of course and also spent time with her father colouring a map of Europe that charted the progress of the Russians and the Allies. They could clearly see the end of the war was near and this excited them, at least a bit, and gave them reason for hope. Of course, they talked about food, what had happened during the war, and what the future might hold. Despite the fact that they caused his five-month ordeal, Peter did not discuss the Dutch Nazis who betrayed him---he believed they were members of Inge's family and, as he loved Inge, he did not want her embarrassment to come between them.

Nearer the end of the war, when hunger became critical for millions of people, the Germans relented somewhat and agreed to allow the Red Cross to bring in some food stuffs as well as white bread (most city residents had not seen any of that for a couple of years). To Peter and Inge it tasted like manna from heaven. Towards the end of April 1945 the Germans also allowed allied Air Forces to pass over certain areas at low level and drop food. Included in the crates were army rations with canned stew, canned soups, chocolate bars, crackers and even cigarettes. By that time cigarettes were worth their weight in gold. My parents can still recall seeing those low level American relief bombers dropping food supplies by parachute or just dumping them out of aircraft. They were all so very grateful to receive these things. The men in the bombers waived at them as they passed over, a sight that was itself quite surreal, but in a good way.

Following is a copy of an article Peter found in a newspaper, the *Venice Herald Tribune*, in Venice, Florida, based on an account by an American pilot, Robert Penny, who flew bombers over Holland to make food drops. For Peter, it is a reminder of what actually happened then:

His mission: Operation Manna, a mid-1945 attempt by American forces to save the Dutch people from starvation. Robert Penny was a member of the 96th bomb group in the Air Force, and flew on a volunteer basis, without armament. The Germans occupied the Netherlands at the time, and the Royal Air Force planned the food drops to stave off the Dutch famine.

"We watched the Germans wheel their .88-millimeter guns into position but they held their fire, since they needed food just as much as the Dutch people did."

Robert Penny served in the 96th Bomb Group, which dropped food in Holland as part of "Operation Manna."

Had it not been for the cease-fire and truce, which allowed these flights to take place, many of the Dutch residents would have died in the hills. Penny, who went into the service in 1943, made 27 rounds over the territory, and let go of thousands of pounds of K-rations from his B-17 aircraft.

After the war, Penny worked as a sales and marketing manager for Warner-Lambert, now Pfizer, a major pharmaceutical company. Now 84, Penny lives in Sarasota with his wife of 62 years, Shirley. The couple is blessed with seven grown children.

'We were involved in something called "Operation Manna" in early spring of 1945. Field Marshal Montgomery of the United Kingdom had cut off northern Holland from the rest of Europe. The German commander in Holland refused to surrender his troops, since the German soldiers were fighting elsewhere.

But by taking this action, he was sentencing not only his troops but also the Dutch people to starvation.

Eisenhower arranged for a temporary truce so that relief supplies could be flown into northern Holland.

In March of 1945, Roosevelt sent a telegram to Churchill, which said: "Limited feeding programs for the Netherlands. The time has arrived when the continued withholding of food from the occupied countries is likely to hurt our friends more than our enemies."

In April, Churchill wrote back: "The plight of the civilian population in occupied Holland is desperate. People are dying daily from starvation. There is need for action to bring immediate help to northern Holland."

The Eighth Air Headquarters issued an order that our bomb group would have to stand down from bombing missions and convert our B-17s to cargo-type planes and fly food to the Dutch people.

We dropped complete meals, similar to K-rations that weighed 450 pounds each. Ours, the 96th bomb group, made five food drops.

At the time of "Operation Manna," we had completed 27 combat missions and were selected to lead the mission to drop food to the Dutch.

Our co-pilot, Commanding Gen. Archie Olds, was awarded the Dutch Flying Cross.

It was dangerous to assemble 36 bombers at 20,000 feet, and it took over two hours to assemble all three squadrons of 12 planes each into formation.

Flying at 1,500 feet in foul weather was much more risky. We dropped to 500 feet to cross the North Sea and one of our planes clipped his left wing on a radar tower at the English coast. Our orders were, "If you don't get shot at, drop the food as planned, from an altitude of 500 feet."

We watched the Germans wheel their .88-millimeter guns into position but they held their fire, since they needed food just as much as the Dutch people did.

We did make the drop on target, and on time, and we returned safely to our base. I can still see the Dutch people and the German soldiers waving to us as we dropped food that saved their lives.

The Dutch people have never forgotten those days of near-starvation. My wife and I visited Amsterdam in 1984 and met people who remembered Operation Manna. The pilot said, "I recall how cold it was and the struggle and fearful feeling it was to fly so low and not get shot at'. We had the joy of giving instead of waiting for death and destruction.[xx]

Below is the "secret" flight path used by Mr. Penny and his fellow airmen.

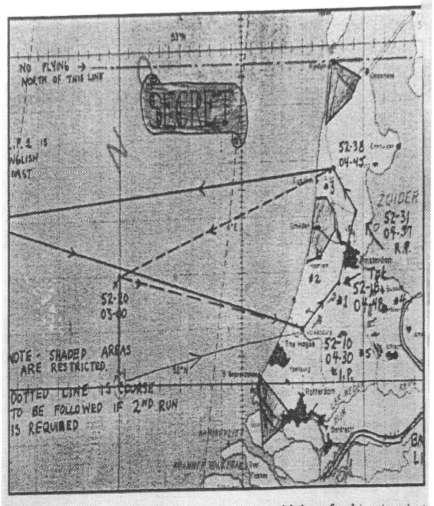

The Luftwaffe honored this route so we could drop food to starving Dutch. (Eichorn)

Flight path for food missions to save the starving Dutch

German leaders in Holland and Allied forces eventually worked out ways to bring in food over land as well, but it would take a long time for the many starving millions to recover after the war was over. Below is a photograph of the official ration city Dutch were forced to live on.[xxi]

Official daily food ration

In the meantime the *ondergrondse* people were organizing an army to take over when the Germans finally capitulated. Peter and Piet had joined the army some time before, and Jacob was a member from the beginning of that force commanded by Prince Bernhard. In secluded locations around Rotterdam they trained with weapons: Stenguns, rifles, hand grenades and so on. No actual firing occurred as that would attract attention. When the official capitulation occurred on May 5, 1945, Peter was on guard duty at a road checkpoint and did not get to see much of the jubilation that gripped the populace.

Of course Dutch elation over the end of war was tempered by the lack of energy many people felt due to months of starvation at the hands of their German occupiers. Maybe the Germans were retaliating against the Dutch resistance; maybe they resented the fact that though they thought of the Dutch as their cultural Aryan brothers, most Dutch did not see things in the orderly German way; maybe it was the use of Dutch intelligence to help in the Allied bombing of Germans in retreat; or maybe it was a combination of these factors or others. The reality is, as Peter recalls it, the Germans had made a deliberate attempt to kill Dutch civilians by starving them to death. They did not succeed; a small triumph for most of them who went on to rebuild and try to carry on a normal life thereafter---"stronger through struggle" as the Rotterdam motto goes.

Chapter Seven

Future

For Peter and Inge and their fellow Dutchmen, the war was over and earnest reconstruction began in Holland and all of physically devastated Europe. Many of the Dutch survivors rounded up to serve in German war industries began to return to Holland, back to their families and pre-enslavement lives. There were various relief agencies at work, and the military apparatus of the Allied forces now focused on rebuilding and rehabilitating blown-apart structures and on food distribution. The Dutch government returned to Holland, and the Queen and her royal family came home.

After the war ended, Peter remembers going a couple of times to the Maas Railway Station in downtown Rotterdam. He saw train car after train car unloading people returning home, liberated from enslavement in Germany. Disembarking, they were met by family or friends some, no doubt, not having been seen or heard from for years. People hugged each other tightly not wanting to let go, many cried with tears of joy and joined in the triumphant atmosphere. Peter believes, however, that these former slave workers were pre-qualified to come back to Holland by Dutch authorities working in Germany or at the border. The Dutch government did not want to let just anyone come into Holland without conducting some verification of their status or eligibility to do so.

The war had also displaced millions of people whom the Germans had sent to death camps or labour camps or wherever they required slaves. Those who survived wanted to come home if they could. But many, of course, did not return to their homelands, including Poles, Russians or Jews who did not want to go back to Stalin's new world order in Poland or Russia. These people were stateless. My parents heard about the death marches many of these fear-saturated peoples were forced by the SS to endure. They heard about the utter squalor of concentration camps. When Peter was in Zwolle before the war ended, fellow-prisoners talked about the death marches. As the eastern front had shrunk in retreat, in bitter cold and horrible conditions fanatical SS troops marched their skeletal prisoners as long as they could until it became obvious they would be overtaken by the Red Army. Then they often fled leaving the prisoners to their own devices, unguarded and in a state of total disarray. It was well known that those German troops who were captured and did not make escape themselves from the Red Army were sent straight to Siberia to live out a well deserved miserable existence there. There was a lot of hatred towards the Germans at the end of the war and, of course, it did not emanate from just the Russians. Incidentally, right after the war, in an act of retribution, Holland sought to annex a small piece of Germany near Kleef (Kleve in German). When the Dutch government realized that this was not such a smart thing to do it returned the territory to Germany. It was spoils of war that did not last too long but may have given some small temporary comfort to an immediate post war desire for revenge.

But other proper acts of retribution happened to Nazis who held power and authority during the war. Anton Mussert, the leader of the Dutch Nazis, was arrested and convicted of treason. He was shot to death by a firing squad in 1946. Seyss-Inquart, Hitler's designate in Holland, was also convicted of serious offences at Nuremberg. He was hanged in 1946. There were also private acts of retribution carried out by Dutch citizens after the war. Can you blame them?

My parents participated in some of the euphoria in Holland as well. There were many street parties, but still not much food to celebrate with, usually just crackers. But it did not matter; they were free of Nazi oppression. That summer of 1945 my parents bicycled to Zwolle just to get away. They rode back to the town where less than half a year earlier Peter and his fellow inmates toiled under their German overseers. Along the way they bought a whole kilo of cherries from a fruit farmer and ate them all. It was heaven. They stopped in Baarne where they stayed with Inge's grandfather who made them cauliflower. They will never forget that he accidentally put sugar in the cauliflower, thinking it was salt. It tasted horrible, but they ate it nonetheless. Elizabeth's expression, "Some day you will want" was still ringing in Peter's ears.

Shortly after the liberation Jacob was invited to come to the Bierbrouwery de Oranjeboom to be greeted and spoken to by their Commander, Prince Bernhard. A big issue then was what would happen to those officers who had voluntarily gone into German captivity. That was a sore point because those people were treated like heroes. They received more tobacco and clothing tickets and were doubly despised for that; some even got promotions. In Jacob's eyes, those officers were tantamount to collaborators, as they did not take the chances that he and others like him took to defend Holland and undermine the German invaders.

In September, 1945, my father started college education at the Technical College of Rotterdam. It was a four-year program which he was able to complete in just three years because of certain credits he received from his high school education. The first year was course work until May, 1946. He then worked from October 1946 to December 1947 for F. van Welzenes, an engineering firm in Rotterdam where he received his practical training. He completed his course work by the spring of 1948 and graduated on July 16, 1948.

Then came another unwelcome surprise: Peter received a military draft notice from the Dutch government, a depressing moment almost like the day he received the *Arbeitseinsatz* summons, though perhaps not so frightful. He attended basic training and was told he would be sent to Indonesia. It was suggested that he choose officer training as that would be easier on him. What irked him greatly was that of the twenty-five members of his graduating class only five were drafted into the army. Those who were not drafted got to further their careers, while he had to get on a slow boat to Indonesia for thirty days starting September 26, 1949, just eleven days after his marriage to Inge. After that trip on the *Volendam* (below), he spent a full year in Indonesia for Queen and country serving Holland's foreign economic interests there under the oppressively hot sun even though that country had declared its independence from Holland in 1945.

The Volendam

My grandparents also lived in Indonesia, in Malang on the island of Java, where Jacob taught school. Jan and Jaap attended high school there. Even his sister Truus was married in Indonesia. Only Piet managed to stay in Holland to further his education. For years Peter suspected that Jacob was behind his being drafted back into the army and ending up in Indonesia but never confronted his father about the matter. However, there is one consolation, Peter learned to play ping pong, a skill he passed on to his children and which gave them years of enjoyment. But he also learned to hate rice. That happens when you get it seven days a week three times a day.

When Peter returned to Holland on November 11, 1950, after yet another thirty days aboard ship, he and Inge decided that their future would not be in that country. He, like many reserve officers, was notified that he would have to report back for duty every year for training. The reality, for him, was that for ten years---five years under the Nazi boot and another five under the Dutch military---he had been told what to do, when to breathe, when to eat, and so on. He was sick of it and needed to get out. They decided to move to Canada in 1951 to make a new start and left their country of birth behind.

That was also the year Jacob met Prince Bernhard who decorated him with the bronze lion medal, the second highest medal for bravery, for his service at Valkenburg Airfield. He was allowed to bring two people to the ceremony, Elizabeth and one of the twins. They were invited to the Royal Palace at Amsterdam. Each recipient was given a hook to wear on their jacket so that the Prince only had to hang a medal on it. Prince Bernhard had apparently done it many times before and he spent about thirty seconds with each recipient. In his diary, Jacob relates that when the Prince saw him he had that look on his face as if he had seen Jacob somewhere before. Jacob replied, "Your Highness, I am a simple teacher. I am no longer in active service and next month I am going to Indonesia again." The Prince asked Jacob how he earned the medal about which he wrote of his reply: "Valkenburg which meant that the lion was already eleven years old, a ripe old age for any lion." It was then that, for the first time, the Prince laughed. When Jacob got back to his seat his family wanted to know what he discussed with Prince Bernhard because he spent more time talking with the Prince than anyone else to which Jacob replied, "We had played marbles together in our youth, we are old friends." Below are the war medals awarded to Jacob that day.

In 1951, my parents sailed for Canada where Peter had been promised a job, only to find out when he arrived that the job did not exist. He had a wife and my oldest brother Jack on the way and he had no money. But, as I have said, he has a tenacious spirit and this obstacle was nothing compared to the ones he had known six years earlier. He overcame it and made a good life for his growing family in a new land.

Jacob and Elizabeth followed to Canada in 1956 and eventually they were joined by all Peter's siblings except Piet. By 1961 the Dutch government had tracked Peter down through its embassy in Ottawa and sent him a letter stating that when he returned to Holland he was to report to a certain army officer! In their eyes he was still in the army even though he had been a Canadian citizen since 1956. Peter did not return to Holland until 1967. Needless to say, he did not report for duty when he travelled there for a holiday.

Peter has told his six children from time to time about Holland before and during the war. He and Inge wanted to forget the war; thus, he tried to keep the narrative of his experiences relatively light. Some of his children may have learned more details than others, but my father has not given a personal account to me until now. His memoir is a legacy of survival in the face of adversity. His decision to flee his Nazi captors on December 25, 1944 is the probable reason he was able to survive the war and have a future with Inge. Peter's little sister Truus and Inge took their lives into their hands looking for him when he was imprisoned and, while he was not happy then about the risks they ran, he is grateful for their effort to come to his aid. At times, he did not think he would ever see Inge again. She has been the light of his life for sixty-seven years and a deeply loved mother to all their children. For that, now and in eternity, he, and all of us, shall be forever grateful.

Endnotes

i   Gebr. Spanjersberg N.V. Rotterdam. These post cards are sixty nine or more years old and were provided by Jacob to Peter. Reprinted with kind permission of Hallmark Cards Nederland

ii   Gebr. Spanjersberg N.V. Rotterdam. *Ibid*

iii   Vogel, Steve, *The Pentagon*, Random House, 2007

iv   Major Norman Philips, *Holland and the Canadians*, The Canada Netherlands Committee, Contact Publishing Company Amsterdam

v   Hansen, Randall, *Fire and Fury The Allied Bombing of German 1942-45*, Doubleday Canada, 2008

vi   *Ibid*

vii   Informatiebulletin No. 29 Augustus 2009 Stichting National Monument Kamp Amersfoort

viii   www.tweede-wereldoorlog.org/petervantoor-kamp

ix   Major Norman Philips, *Holland and the Canadians*, The Canada Netherlands Committee, Contact Publishing Company Amsterdam

x   Hitchcock, William I., *The Bitter Road to Freedom, Simon & Shuster 2008*

xi   Hitchcock, William I., *The Bitter Road to Freedom, Simon & Shuster 2008*

xii   Major Norman Philips, *Holland and the Canadians*, The Canada Netherlands Committee, Contact Publishing Company Amsterdam

xiii   http://www.v2rocket.com/start/deployment/denhaag.html

xiv   Hansen, Randall, *Fire and Fury The Allied Bombing of German 1942-45*, Doubleday Canada, 2008

xv   http://www.reisenett.no/map_collection/europe/Netherlands.jpg

xvi   Hitchcock, William I., *The Bitter Road to Freedom, Simon & Shuster 2008*

xvii Hitchcock, William I. *The Bitter Road to Freedom Simon & Shuster 2008*

xviii Hitchcock, William I. *The Bitter Road to Freedom Simon & Shuster 2008*

xix   Major Norman Philips, *Holland and the Canadians*, The Canada Netherlands Committee, Contact Publishing Company Amsterdam

xx   With gracious permission from *Venice Herald-Tribune*, February 20, 2009, p. 4B, Abbey Weingarten and Mr. Robert Penny

xxi   Major Norman Philips, Holland and the Canadians, The Canada Netherlands Committee, Contact Publishing Company Amsterdam

About The Author

Robert J. van Kessel is a practicing lawyer and textbook author in the fields of insolvency, financial recovery and civil litigation. He is married and has three sons attending university.